God's Providence

Presented to
Jack Hare

by Forest Fold Sunday School on behalf of Ron Bishop during Lockdown 2020

In God whose Word I praise, in God I trust; I shall not be afraid Psalm. 56 v 4

God's Providence

BY SALLY MICHAEL

P.O. BOX 817 • PHILLIPSBURG • NEW JERSEY 08865-0817

© 2013 text by Sally Michael, illustrations by Fred Apps

All rights reserved. No part of this book may be reproduced, stored in a retrieval system, or transmitted in any form or by any means—electronic, mechanical, photocopy, recording, or otherwise—except for brief quotations for the purpose of review or comment, without the prior permission of the publisher, P&R Publishing Company, P.O. Box 817, Phillipsburg, New Jersey 08865–0817.

Unless otherwise indicated, Scripture quotations are from *ESV Bible* ® (*The Holy Bible, English Standard Version* ®). Copyright © 2001 by Crossway Bibles, a publishing ministry of Good News Publishers. Used by permission. All rights reserved.

ISBN: 978-1-59638-714-0 (pbk)
ISBN: 978-1-59638-715-7 (ePub)
ISBN: 978-1-59638-716-4 (Mobi)

Page design and typesetting by Dawn Premako

Printed in the United States of America

Dedicated to my parents,
Richard and Lucile Fregeau.

When I look at God's acts of providence in your lives,
I stand in awe of our great God!

I am God, and there is no other;
I am God, and there is none like me,
declaring the end from the beginning
and from ancient times things not yet done,
saying, "My counsel shall stand,
and I will accomplish all my purpose,"
calling a bird of prey from the east,
the man of my counsel from a far country.
I have spoken, and I will bring it to pass;
I have purposed, and I will do it.
—Isaiah 46:9–11

The Lord of hosts has sworn:
"As I have planned,
so shall it be,
and as I have purposed,
so shall it stand."
—Isaiah 14:24

Contents

Preface 10

Introduction: How to Use This Book 12

1. No One Is Like God 16
2. God Is Watching and Working 20
3. God Keeps the World Going 24
4. God Rules Well 28
5. God Has a Plan for the World 32
6. God Has a Good Reason for What He Does 36
7. God Does What He Plans 40
8. God Is Never Surprised 44
9. God Knows What He Is Doing 48
10. All for His Glory 52
11. God Rules over Nature 56
12. God Rules over Life 60
13. God Rules over Rulers and Countries 64
14. God Rules over His Word 68
15. God Rules over Man's Heart 72

16. God Rules over the Cross 76

17. God Rules over Salvation 80

18. God Rules over Evil 84

19. God Rules over Suffering 88

20. God Rules over Man's Way 92

21. God Rules over Circumstances 96

22. God's Plans Work Perfectly 100

23. All Things Work for Good 104

24. Trusting God's Heart 108

25. Trusting God's Will 112

26. See God at Work 116

God Moves in a Mysterious Way 120

WESTMINSTER LARGER CATECHISM (1647)
Question 18

Question: What are God's works of providence?

Answer: God's works of providence are His most holy, wise, and powerful preserving and governing all His creatures; ordering them, and all their actions, to His own glory.

HEIDELBERG CATECHISM (1563)
Question 27

Question: What then is the providence of God?

Answer: The almighty and everywhere present power of God, whereby, as it were, by His hand, He still upholds heaven and earth, with all creatures, and so governs them that herbs and grass, rain and drought, fruitful and barren years, meat and drink, health and sickness, riches and poverty, yea, all things, come not by chance, but by His fatherly hand.

> God's eye is watching and His hand is working
> to sustain and rule the world
> to work out all His plans . . .
> for His glory
> and the good of His children.

Preface

The Lord has established his throne in the heavens, and his kingdom rules over all. —Psalm 103:19

God's throne is in the heavens . . . and He rules over all. Everything is under His sovereign control. Every person, every circumstance, every action . . . every single thing is subject to God's eternal plan for this world. He is at work in the world every day, moving all of history to fulfill His purposes. History is *His* story—His story of *Creation*, *Fall*, *Redemption*, and *Return*. Every piece has been carefully orchestrated by Him and will be brought to perfect completion. What a staggering truth this is. This is the doctrine of the providence of God.

Can a child understand this? In the pages of this book you will find the words to explain this incredibly important doctrine to your child. As the Creator and Owner of this world, God has the right to rule it, and He has the power, wisdom, and goodness to rule it well. Beginning with these simple truths, you will form with your child a simple definition of the providence of God, specifically that

> God's eye is watching and His hand is working
> to sustain and rule the world
> to work out all His plans . . .
> for His glory
> and the good of His children.

If a child can understand and embrace God's providence over all things, he can rest in God's sovereign care for him. How many fears, worries, frustrations, and tears will a child be spared by truly understanding and bowing to God's wisdom? How many circumstances will be embraced with childlike trust by seeing God's hand in the everyday occurrences of life? How much grace and peace will come with the understanding that through suffering God conforms us to the image of His Son?

How reassuring is the doctrine of the providence of God! It focuses our eyes on God and establishes our trust in His providential hand in the universe, and it leads us to worship Him as we see the pieces of His eternal plan fall into place. What an amazing God we have—one who rules over all things, big and small, with power, wisdom, and love! How great is our God, who works all things for His glory and the good of His children!

> Your way, O God, is holy.
>   What god is great like our God?
> You are the God who works wonders;
>   you have made known your might among the peoples. (Psalm 77:13–14)

> For as high as the heavens are above the earth,
>   so great is his steadfast love toward those who fear him. (Psalm 103:11)

Introduction
How to Use This Book

This book was written to give parents an opportunity to present solid truth to their children and to encourage real-life application of the truth.

Relational

Children receive more encouragement to learn when truth is presented by a trusted individual. Your positive, relational parent-child commitment will be a real benefit when you sit down together to read this book. Your time together over the Word should be positive, affirming, and loving.

Interactive

There is a greater impact when an individual discovers truth, instead of just hearing it presented. Many questions have been incorporated into the text of this book to encourage your child to wonder and think critically. The process of discovery will be circumvented if you don't give your child adequate time to think and respond. After asking a question, wait for a response. If your child has difficulty, ask the question in a different way or give a few hints.

Questions and responses can be springboards for more questions and discovery as you interact with your child's mind and heart. The Holy Spirit is the real teacher, so depend on Him to give both you and your child thoughts and truths to explore together, and to bring the necessary understanding. Take the time to work through each story at a leisurely pace—giving time for interaction and further dialogue. The goal should be to get the material into the child, not just to get the child through the material.

Understandable

These stories have been written with attention given to explaining difficult or potentially new concepts. Some of these concepts may take time for your child to digest. Allow your child to ponder new truths. Read the story more than once, allowing the truth to be better understood and integrated into your child's theological framework. At times, have your child read parts of the lesson, giving an opportunity for visual learning.

Because vocabulary can be child-specific, define the particular words foreign to your child. Retell difficult sections in familiar wording, and ask questions to be sure your child understands the truth being taught.

Theological

More than just acquainting your child with the providence of God, this book is building a foundation of biblical theology for your child. As your child begins to correctly understand who God is and how He interacts with the world, he or she won't just have a vague notion of God, but will be able to relate to the God of the Bible.

Because the Word of God has convicting and converting power, Bible texts are quoted word-for-word in some parts. Some of these verses may be beyond the child's understanding, so you may need to explain unfamiliar words or thoughts. Even though clear comprehension may be difficult, hearing the Word itself is a means the Holy Spirit often uses to encourage faith in your child (Romans 10:17). Do not minimize the effectual influence of God's Word in the tender souls of children.

Since the Word of God is living and active, allow the child to read the actual Bible verses as much as possible. Also, encourage your child to memorize some of the verses so he or she can meditate on them at other times.

The gospel is presented numerous times throughout the book. Use this as an opportunity to share God's work of grace in your life, and to converse with your child about his or her spiritual condition. Be careful not to confuse spiritual interest with converting faith, and take care to avoid giving premature assurances. Fan the flames of gospel-inspired conviction and tenderness toward the sacrificial love of Jesus without prematurely encouraging your child to pray "the sinner's prayer."[1]

Application

Understanding the truth is essential, but understanding it alone is insufficient. Truth must also be embraced in the heart and acted upon in daily life. Often, children cannot make the connection between a biblical truth and real-life application, so you, the parent, must help bridge the gap.

Consider the following quotation from D. Martyn Lloyd-Jones:

> We must always put things in the right order, and it is Truth first. . . . The heart is always to be influenced through the understanding—the mind, then the heart, then the will. . . . But God forbid that anyone should think that it ends with the intellect. It starts there, but it goes on. It then moves the heart and finally the man yields his will. He obeys, not grudgingly or unwillingly, but with the whole heart. The Christian life is a glorious perfect life that takes up and captivates the entire personality.[2]

Spend a few days or even a week on each story. Reread the story, discuss the truths, and follow the suggestions in the Learning to Trust God section. Most importantly, help your child to see that God is who He says He is, and help him

---

1. Some excellent resources for parents regarding the salvation of children can be found at www.childrendesiringgod.org. Resources include the following: a booklet titled *Helping Children Understand the Gospel* and two seminars from the 2007 Children Desiring God conference, How Great a Salvation—"Leading Children to a Solid Faith" and "Presenting the Gospel to Children."
2. D. Martyn Lloyd-Jones, *Spiritual Depression* (Grand Rapids: William B. Eerdmans, 1965), 61–62.

or her to act in response to the truth. Point out God's involvement in daily life, and thank Him for being a God of amazing providences.

Prayer

Ultimately, our efforts are effective only if the Holy Spirit breathes on our teaching and quickens it to the heart. Pray not only before going through the stories, but also in the succeeding days, that your child would see God's character expressed in His providence over the world and respond in faith to Him.

No One Is Like God

Have you ever made a paper airplane? Paper airplanes are great—but they are only made of paper and can't compare to real airplanes. It would be silly to even try to compare the two. A real airplane is so much greater than a paper airplane.

That is the way it is with God. God is so much greater than anyone or anything else. No one and nothing compares with God. God is bigger, stronger, greater, smarter, better than anyone or anything else!

Do you know how big God is? This is the Bible's way of helping us to understand how big God is:

> Who has measured the waters in the hollow of his hand
>   and marked off the heavens with a span . . . ? (Isaiah 40:12)

Cup your hand, holding it open and curling your fingers. See the little spot in the middle? That is called the hollow. All the waters of the world—all the oceans, rivers, and lakes—can be held in the hollow of God's hand. That's how big God is!

Now hold your hand open. The distance between your thumb and the little finger is called a span. Measure around the outside of this book with your handspan. How many spans does it take? In only one span of God's hand He measures the sky, all the planets and stars, the whole universe!

When you were little, you had to learn so many things—how to walk and talk, tie your shoe, add 2+2, ride a bike. . . . What about God?

> Whom did he consult,
>   and who made him understand?
> Who taught him the path of justice,

> and taught him knowledge,
> and showed him the way of understanding? (Isaiah 40:14)

No one taught God anything—He has always known it all! Just think of the things that God knows. He knows everything that has happened in history and everything that will happen tomorrow, next year, and forever. He knows how many grains of sand are on every beach, He knows every bird that flies in the air or falls to the earth, and He knows the cure to every disease.

What are you thinking about right now? God knows it! And He knows every thought you will ever think—all your thoughts, your mother's, your teacher's, and the thoughts of every ruler of every country! He knows how many hairs you have on your head and every word you will ever say. What other things can you think of that God knows? No one knows what God knows! He is greater than anyone or anything else. Guess what He knows about the stars?

> Lift up your eyes on high and see:
> who created these?
> He who brings out their host by number,
> calling them all by name,
> by the greatness of his might,

> and because he is strong in power
> not one is missing. (Isaiah 40:26)

Wow! God knows the name of every one of the trillions and trillions of stars! He shows them off every night . . . and never loses even one of them! That is how powerful God is!

Who or what could possibly compare to the Almighty God?

> To whom then will you liken God,
> or what likeness compare with him?
> An idol! A craftsman casts it,
> and a goldsmith overlays it with gold
> and casts for it silver chains.
> He who is too impoverished for an offering
> chooses wood that will not rot;
> he seeks out a skillful craftsman
> to set up an idol that will not move. (Isaiah 40:18–20)

You could try to make your own god. But it would just sit there. It could not move or do anything. It would not be anything like the one true God, who did not have to be made, who always was, who lives forever and will never wear out, who speaks, acts, and works in the world. Only God is God.

> Do you not know? Do you not hear?
> Has it not been told you from the beginning?
> Have you not understood from the foundations of the earth?
> It is he who sits above the circle of the earth,
> and its inhabitants are like grasshoppers;
> who stretches out the heavens like a curtain,
> and spreads them like a tent to dwell in. (Isaiah 40:21–22)

What does the Bible say that people are like in comparison to God? Grasshoppers! Little, unimportant grasshoppers! God made the whole world and takes care of everything in it. God is so great that, compared to Him, we are like grasshoppers.

Our God is a GREAT GOD! We should sing and shout from the highest mountaintops about how great He is. Only God is God. Only God is most great! No one and nothing can be compared to God.

> I am God, and there is no other;
>   I am God, and there is none like me. (Isaiah 46:9)

LEARNING TO TRUST GOD

✢ Read Isaiah 40:12–26. What else do these verses tell you about the greatness of God?

✢ What things do people get so excited about that they shout about them? What does Isaiah 40:9 tell us to shout about? What good news of God's greatness can you tell to someone else?

✢ *Activity:* All of nature shouts about the greatness of God. With your family, carefully observe something in nature. Draw a detailed picture of what you see. What does this part of God's creation tell you about God? Start a nature notebook with drawings that shout about God's greatness.

God Is Watching and Working

When was the last time you were sick? How long were you sick? Can you imagine what it would be like to be sick for 38 years?

The Bible tells us about a man who was sick this long. His problem was in his legs. They didn't work, so he couldn't walk. The man was lying by a pool with a lot of other sick people when Jesus showed up. Other people just walked by this man. Some probably didn't even notice him—but not Jesus. Jesus *saw* him. He saw the legs that didn't work. He saw the 38 years of suffering, and he saw the heart of the man.

Jesus didn't just see the man and then look away. He spoke to the man and *did* something to help him. He healed the man's sick legs so he could walk again. There is none like God. Only God who heals sick legs is most great!

This should have made the people happy and ready to praise God. But instead they were mad—mad because Jesus healed on the day of worship.

> But Jesus answered them, "My Father is working until now, and I am working." (John 5:17)

Did you know that God works? God's job is to take care of the whole world! God didn't just create the world and then ignore it. He is always watching over His world. He *sees* everything in the world—every blade of grass, every grain of sand, every joy and sorrow, every single person. And He is always working in the world, always *doing* things—making flowers grow, keeping the stars in the sky, turning winter into spring, making your lungs breathe in and out, and trillions and trillions of other things all the time. God is always at work doing things in the world.

This is called God's *providence*—His seeing and doing in the world. The word *providence* might seem hard to understand, but there is an easy way to understand the providence of God. Just think about an eye and a hand. God's eye is watching over the world. His hand is at work in the world. This is what *providence* means. The Bible talks about the "eyes" of God and the "hand" of God[1]:

The eyes of the Lord are in every place,
    keeping watch on the evil and the good. (Proverbs 15:3)

God's eyes are watching over the whole world, seeing everything that happens—every bird that falls, every tear that is cried, every problem, every person, every smile, and every song.

O Lord God, you have only begun to show your servant your greatness and your mighty hand. For what god is there in heaven or on earth who can do such works and mighty acts as yours? (Deuteronomy 3:24)

In His seeing, God is also doing. He is doing trillions

---

1. God is a spirit and does not have a physical body, but the Bible uses words like "eye" and "hand" to help us to understand who God is and what He does in the world.

of things—mighty acts every day that we don't even know about. He is at work in everything that happens in the world.

Have you ever watched your mother cook gravy or pudding? She watches it—to be sure the burner is hot enough, to see if it is boiling or starting to thicken. She is also doing something—stirring it to keep it from burning, turning the burner down if it is too hot, and taking it off the stove when it is done. Your mother is watching and working, seeing and doing.

This is what God does in the world. He is always watching and working, seeing and doing. Every story in the Bible shows us this is true. When God sent the flood, He kept Noah, his family, and the animals safe in the ark. He was watching them all the time and working for them—protecting them from the storm, keeping the boat from sinking, giving them air to breathe. He didn't just send the flood and forget about Noah and the animals.

> But God remembered Noah and all the beasts and all the livestock that were with him in the ark. And God made a wind blow over the earth, and the waters subsided. (Genesis 8:1)

Where do you see God's "eye" and "hand" in this verse? What did God see? He saw Noah and the animals with eyes of tender love and care for them. What did God do? He sent a wind to dry up the waters so they could get out of the ark and onto dry land.

God is always watching and working. This is His providence—His seeing and doing. When you read the Bible, think about God's eye and hand, His seeing and doing. You will find it all over the Bible. And if you look around you, you will see it everywhere in the world. Every day, in everything, God is watching and working. Ask Him to open your eyes to His providence.

> From of old no one has heard
>   or perceived by the ear,

no eye has seen a God besides you,
   who acts for those who wait for him. (Isaiah 64:4)

LEARNING TO TRUST GOD

✢ Read a story from the Bible. Where do you see God's eye and hand? This is God's providence—His seeing and doing.

✢ Read Isaiah 64:4. What does this tell you about God? What are some things God has done for your family? Thank Him for His providence over your family.

✢ *Activity:* Make a bookmark with an eye and hand on it. Put it in your Bible to remind you to look for what God sees and does. Is there a need God has shown your family? Is there something you can do about it?

God Keeps the World Going

What things can you think of that are very powerful? Maybe you're thinking about the blast of a rocket or a nuclear bomb. They are both very powerful. But think of how much more powerful this was: "Let there be light . . ." And there was light! "Let there be . . ." land and trees, stars and animals, and man! God's voice is powerful! There is none like God!

But God did not just create the world and then leave it alone. If He had, there would be no world now. God is still "providing" for the world. Every day the sun comes up in the morning, the stars are in the sky, and rain waters the earth. Year after year, seeds grow into flowers that make more seeds that grow into more flowers. Winter always comes after fall, and spring comes after winter. God does all this and more! God is actively providing for and taking care of the world. He keeps it going day after day, year after year . . . for thousands of years.

When God created the world, it was like a quick blast on a whistle. He spoke, and the world came into being. But God's work in keeping the world going is like a hum that doesn't stop. It is always there, always quietly at work. This is called God's *sustaining providence*.

What two things help you to understand God's providence? If you said "an eye and a hand," you are right. God's eye is watching over the world; God's hand is at work in the world. God is always seeing and doing. And one of the things He is doing is keeping the world going, or *sustaining* it. Just like a constant hum.

> For by him all things were created, in heaven and on earth, visible and invisible, whether thrones or dominions or rulers or authorities—all things were created through him and for him. And he is before all things, and in him all things hold together. (Colossians 1:16–17)

God holds the world together every day. Everything in creation is a message to us about God's sustaining providence—about God keeping the world going and holding it together. Every morning when the sun comes up, it reminds us that God is watching over us. When the stars come out at night, it is like God saying, "I am still here." When thunder, lightning, strong wind, and rain appear, it is God showing us that He is powerful. The rain is God providing water for us to drink and to water the plants so that we have food to eat. Every time winter follows fall and spring follows winter, God reminds us, "I am unchanging. You can count on me."

If you dropped a book, would it fall up or down? Every time you drop something and it falls down instead of up, it is a reminder that gravity still works and God is holding the world together. He keeps order in the world so that gravity stays the same and keeps working every time.

How long can you hold a hum? Try it. Can you hold it until the end of this story? Until the end of the day? For a week . . . or a month . . . or a year? God holds His "hum" of keeping the world together until the end of time. He does not need to take a breath, get a drink of water, sleep, or get more energy. God keeps the world going because He is all-powerful!

God also holds together all living things.

> Can you hunt the prey for the lion,
>   or satisfy the appetite of the young lions,
> when they crouch in their dens
>   or lie in wait in their thicket?
> Who provides for the raven its prey,
>   when its young ones cry to God for help,
>   and wander about for lack of food? (Job 38:39–41)

God gives the animals their food. He shows them how and where to hunt. He gives them (and keeps giving them) the instinct to hunt.

God also holds together the life of every person.

> In him we live and move and have our being. (Acts 17:28)

If God were to take His providing hand away from our lungs, we would stop breathing.[1] Every breath we take is a gift from God, who is good and always caring for His world.

Some people say they do not need God. Why is this a foolish thing to say?

Without God's sustaining providence—God's keeping the world going—we would all die. The sun would no longer shine. The waters would dry up. There would be no air, and our lives would stop. All people need God every minute of every day—even if they don't think they do.

God could have made the world and then walked away. But He didn't, because He is good. He provides for His world every day and keeps it going year after year. His hum is still going . . .

---

1. Psalm 104:29

The steadfast love of the LORD never ceases;
> his mercies never come to an end;
they are new every morning;
> great is your faithfulness. (Lamentations 3:22–23)

LEARNING TO TRUST GOD

✢ Read Psalm 104. What reasons does this psalm give you to praise God?

✢ Read Lamentations 3:22–23 again. Make a list with your family of ways God shows us His goodness by keeping the world going.

✢ *Activity:* With your family, make a poster or a book illustrating Psalm 104.

God Rules Well

Are you still humming? No. You probably stopped long ago. But God's "hum" did not stop—like a hum that does not end, His care for the world continues . . . without stopping.

God created the world, and He keeps it going. But that isn't all that God does.

The Lord has established his throne in the heavens,
    and his kingdom rules over all. (Psalm 103:19)

God "rules" the world, like a king rules His country. That means He is in charge. He tells the world what to do. He tells the sun when to get up, the sea where to stop, and the mountain goats when to have baby goats. God tells the rain when to rain, where to rain, and how much to rain. He tells birds, like eagles, to build nests and tells the lightning where to strike. He tells winter when to start and when to end, and the spring flowers when to bloom.[1] **And they all have to obey Him because He is in charge.**

Why do you think God gets to be in charge of the universe?

Maybe this will help you to know the answer. If you color a picture in a coloring book or make a paper airplane, who decides what to do with it? You do. Why? Because it is yours; it belongs to you; you made it.

Who made the world? Yes, God did. And because He made it, God owns the world; it belongs to Him. So He gets to tell the world and everything in it what to do. He has the *right* to rule the world because He is the Owner of the world.

Do you think that God is strong enough to rule the world—to tell the sun every day when to get up, to tell the flowers when to bloom—in every country of

---

1. Job 38:8–13; 39:1–2; 38:35–37, 34; 39:27; 36:30–33; Daniel 2:21

the world? Is God strong enough to tell the rain when to make a flood, to control every wave in every ocean, and to keep the earth from crashing into the sun? It takes a very big and powerful God to rule everything, all the time. But our God is more than big enough to rule the whole world!

> Yours, O Lord, is the greatness and the power and the glory and the victory and the majesty, for all that is in the heavens and in the earth is yours. Yours is the kingdom, O Lord, and you are exalted as head above all. Both riches and honor come from you, and you rule over all. In your hand are power and might, and in your hand it is to make great and to give strength to all. (1 Chronicles 29:11–12)

God's strong hand is working in the world—He fills His hand with lightning and throws it to earth, telling it exactly where to go.[2] **And He never misses. He always hits the target.** The lightning can't decide to go somewhere else, because God is in charge. He has the *right* and the *power* to rule the world.

2. Job 36:32; 37:3

But how do we know that God isn't making a whole bunch of mistakes in running the world? Look around you. Do the tree roots ever grow on the top of the tree? No. Every tree root grows down. God doesn't make mistakes. When you drop something, does it ever fall up instead of down? Do you float off the ground? No. God keeps things falling down and keeps us on the ground. He doesn't make mistakes.[3]

Does the sun come out at night or the sky rain hotdogs instead of raindrops? Does God forget to make winter end or forget to tell the birds to stop growing? No, giant birds don't take over the world and frogs don't start flying. What other wrong or silly things don't happen?

These things don't happen because God keeps everything in His world working right. He knows how to rule the world. He doesn't make any mistakes or stop paying attention, go to sleep, or leave for vacation. God is good at being in charge.

> It is he who made the earth by his power,
> > who established the world by his wisdom,
> > and by his understanding stretched out the heavens.
> > > (Jeremiah 10:12)

If God is smart or wise enough to make the world from nothing, He is wise enough to rule it well. Our God is so great! He has the *right* and *power* and *wisdom* to *rule the world* perfectly.

Can you trust Him to be in charge? Can you trust Him to know what to do in the world, and in your family?

---

3. We will address the mistakes that people sometimes *think* God has made in his creation in a later chapter.

LEARNING TO TRUST GOD

+ Read Genesis 1. What does this tell you about God's right, power, and wisdom to rule the world?

+ Read Job 37–39. What are some things in these verses that show the greatness of God?

+ *Activity:* Clean out some closets and drawers. Make a pile of items that you no longer need. Sort the items into giveaway piles. The owner of each item decides what to do with it. Then bless others with things you no longer need.

God Has a Plan for the World

What is your plan for tomorrow? Where will you go? What will you do? Maybe you plan to go to school or to a soccer game. But you don't know if you really will. You might get sick . . . or it might rain and the soccer game will be cancelled. You can plan, but you can't be sure that your plans will happen.

But God rules the world, and His plans always happen exactly as He has planned them—every time, in every place. Whatever God has decided to do, He does.

> The counsel of the Lord stands forever,
> the plans of his heart to all generations. (Psalm 33:11)

God has a plan for the world—every day of every year for all time. He had a plan for the beginning of the world, and He has a plan for the end of the world and all the time in between. God planned for Moses to be born, for birds to feed Elijah in the wilderness, for Jesus to be born in Bethlehem, and for Paul to write his letter to the Philippians from jail.

God's plan for the world is like a story—it has a beginning, middle, and end. There are different people in the story, and God, the Storyteller, has written a part for each person in the story.

The beginning of God's story of the world is *Creation*, when God made the world and everything in it. Every day of the world's story was written even before God made the world. So God knew just what would happen in the garden of Eden, where Adam and Eve would disobey Him and eat the forbidden fruit. That part of the story is called the *Fall*. The Fall brought sin and death into God's story, but the Fall didn't surprise God because He is the Writer of the story.

And it didn't mess up God's story. It was part of God's plan for the world. God already knew what to do about sin before there was any sin! God had already written the chapter about Jesus coming to earth to die for the sins of men before Adam and Eve sinned.

God sent His Son Jesus to earth to take care of the sin problem. God's plan to take care of the sin problem is called *Redemption*. Jesus knew why He came to earth—what He was supposed to do.

I must preach the good news of the kingdom of God to the other towns as well; for I was sent for this purpose. (Luke 4:43)

Now is my soul troubled. And what shall I say? "Father, save me from this hour"? But for this purpose I have come to this hour. (John 12:27)

Jesus knew His part in God's story of the world. He came to tell men that they could be saved from their sins, and He came to die for the sins of men. He knew God's plan, and He did everything His Father sent

Him to earth to do. Everything written in the history of the world about Jesus happened just as God planned it.

God has a plan for the end of the world too. Someday Jesus will come back to earth. That is called the *Return*. Everyone will know that He is the Son of God, and they will bow down to Jesus, the King of Kings, when He returns.

> Therefore God has highly exalted him and bestowed on him the name that is above every name, so that at the name of Jesus every knee should bow, in heaven and on earth and under the earth, and every tongue confess that Jesus Christ is Lord, to the glory of God the Father. (Philippians 2:9–11)

When Jesus comes back to earth, He will defeat all His enemies. He will crush Satan and evil, and He will throw Satan and all his demons into hell. Everyone who is not trusting in Jesus will follow them into hell.

But best of all, Jesus will gather all those who trust in Him and bring them to Heaven with Him. What a glorious day that will be! Then God will create a new heavens and a new earth and start a new story. What a wonderful plan God has for His children and for His world. All this will happen just as God has planned.

God, the Creator and Ruler of this world, is the One writing the story of the world. History is *His* story—His story of *Creation*, *Fall*, *Redemption*, and *Return*. God's plan won't change, and every part of God's plan will happen as He has planned it.

God has a plan for you too—a part for you to play in His story of the world. You don't know His plan, but God does. Every day of your life was planned even before you were born! What a great, planning God we have! He doesn't leave anything to "just happen," but He has made great and glorious plans for the world. And every single one of them will happen just as He has planned.

Your eyes saw my unformed substance;
in your book were written, every one of them,
    the days that were formed for me,
    when as yet there was none of them. (Psalm 139:16)

The counsel of the LORD stands forever,
    the plans of his heart to all generations. (Psalm 33:11)

LEARNING TO TRUST GOD

✣ Read Psalm 139. What does this tell you about God and His greatness and His plans?

✣ Read Philippians 2:5–11. What do these verses tell you about who Jesus is? (Talk about His identity and His character.)

✣ *Activity:* With your mom or dad, make a timeline of the important events of your life. This is your history. How was God at work in your life? What did He do for you? What does this show you about whether you can trust Him?

God Has a Good Reason for What He Does

What tools does your father have in the garage or your mother have in the kitchen? Each one has a purpose. A screwdriver is useful for putting in and taking out screws; a peeler is useful for removing the peels from potatoes and apples. Each tool has a purpose.

Everything God has made He made with a purpose too. And He has a purpose for everything He does. He created clouds to carry rain and the sun to give light and warmth. He sent the flood to judge evil men, and He sent the wind to open the Red Sea so the Israelites could escape from the soldiers of Pharaoh. He made Pharaoh the ruler of Egypt to show His power in the plagues and to show the greatness of His name.[1] And He sent Jesus to earth to die on the cross to save men from their sin.

> The Lord has made everything for its purpose,
>   even the wicked for the day of trouble. (Proverbs 16:4)

God's eye is watching and His hand is working in the world every day. He keeps the world going and He rules over everything. Everything serves God's purposes; everything in the world works according to His plan. Nothing "just happens." When you flip a coin in the air to see if it lands as "heads" or "tails," you don't control what happens—it is decided by God. If we make plans, they will only work out for us if they are God's plans first. If our plans are not God's plans, they won't happen.

1. Exodus 9:16

The lot is cast into the lap,
> but its every decision is from the Lord. (Proverbs 16:33)

The heart of man plans his way,
> but the Lord establishes his steps. (Proverbs 16:9)

Sometimes we think we know what is best, but there is so much we don't know that only God knows. Why does God do what He does? No one can really know God's purposes. We can only guess. We can see only part of God's plan. But we do know this—when God does something, it is always for a good reason.

When you see a storm, do you know why God sent it?

He loads the thick cloud with moisture;
> the clouds scatter his lightning.
> They turn around and around
> by his guidance,
> to accomplish all that he commands them
> on the face of the habitable world.
> Whether for correction or for his land
> or for love, he causes it to happen. (Job 37:11–13)

Sometimes God sends storms to discipline—like when He sent the flood to judge the world but saved Noah and his family. The story of the flood helps us to remember that we must obey God and follow His ways. It reminds us that if we do not trust in Jesus to give us a new heart, our own hearts will turn away from God and lead us to eternal punishment. Isn't it good that God sent the flood? Isn't it a good warning to us?

Sometimes God causes storms because He knows the land needs water so that plants and trees can grow. Even though we may want to play outside, it is good that God sends rain to water the earth. He sends rain because He loves us—to give us water to drink and plants that grow. Isn't God good? He does everything for a good reason. Everything He does is right.

Do you think you would know which days to send rain and which days to send only sun? Would you know how much rain to send or where to send it? Would you be selfish and send sunny days when you want to do something outside, instead of sending the rain the world needs?

Do you know when people need to have a warning so they will turn away from wrong and when they need to understand God's love? Would you punish the world in love or just because you are angry? Would you do good only to those who are good, and not to those who are mean to you? Even in God's anger, He loves the world. God shows kindness to undeserving sinners, sending His rain and His sun on both good people and evil people.[2]

Only God, the Creator, has the right and the power and the wisdom and the *goodness* to rule the world well. Can you trust God to rule the world well? Do you believe that He *always* has a good reason for what He does—even when you don't like what is happening? Will you tell everyone that God is good and everything He does is right?

> For I will proclaim the name of the LORD;
>   ascribe greatness to our God!

2. Matthew 5:45

"The Rock, his work is perfect,
    for all his ways are justice.
A God of faithfulness and without iniquity,
    just and upright is he." (Deuteronomy 32:3–4)

LEARNING TO TRUST GOD

✢ Read Deuteronomy 32:3–4 again and explain it to your mother or father. Read together Deuteronomy 31:1–22. How does this help you to understand Deuteronomy 32:3–4 better?

✢ Read Ephesians 1:11. What is the inheritance that God has promised to His children? What does it mean that God "works all things according to the counsel of his will"? What is happening in your life right now that you need to trust that God is doing in love? Thank Him for His power, wisdom, and goodness.

✢ *Activity:* How can your family "proclaim the name of the Lord"? What can you do to show that He is good? Think of something your family can do to "proclaim the name of the Lord," and then do it.

God Does What He Plans

Have you ever planned to do something but then couldn't do it? One day you might wake up and say, "Today I am going to ride my bike ten miles!" But all kinds of things could happen to stop you from doing that. You could start to feel sick after breakfast, or storm clouds could roll in, or you could ride five miles and find that you are too tired to ride five miles more. All kinds of things can happen to stop our plans.

But nothing stops God's plans. He doesn't get sick or tired. He doesn't have any of the weaknesses we have. And He is never surprised by storms—or by anything—because He controls all things. So nothing can stop God's plans.

> The Lord of hosts has sworn:
> "As I have planned,
>   so shall it be,
> and as I have purposed,
>   so shall it stand." (Isaiah 14:24)

God planned to send Jonah to Nineveh to preach to the people there. His purpose was to save the evil men of Nineveh and show the greatness of His name. Jonah didn't like God's plan. So Jonah tried to stop God's plan and change God's purposes. He got on a ship that would take him *away* from Nineveh. He tried to run away from God, but no one can run from God or stop His purposes.

God sent a storm on the sea that was so bad it would break apart the ship. The sailors wondered why the storm had come upon them. Who could have made the gods angry? The Bible says that they "cast lots"—that is like drawing straws to see who gets the shortest—and God caused the lot to fall on Jonah. The storm came because Jonah was running from the God of Israel, the one true God. The sailors saw that "the gods" didn't send the storm, but the one true God sent it.

What happened next in God's story of the world and of Jonah and Nineveh? The sailors threw Jonah into the sea and God, the Ruler of the world and all the seas and storms, caused the storm to stop and the sea to become calm.

What would Jonah do now? Jonah was not in control in the middle of the sea, God was. God is always in control. He planned that a fish would swallow Jonah and then spit him up on dry land three days later. Everything serves God's purposes—even fish . . . and disobedient prophets like Jonah. Jonah did go and preach to Nineveh—just like God planned. And the people of Nineveh did repent and come to see God as great and glorious, because God always does what He plans.

The LORD of hosts has sworn:
"As I have planned,
so shall it be,
and as I have purposed,
so shall it stand." (Isaiah 14:24)

Can you think of another time when someone tried to stop God's purposes and change His plans? What about Herod? What did he do? When Herod found out that Jesus had been born, he ordered his soldiers to kill all the baby boys in Bethlehem who were two years old or younger. What an evil thing to do! Herod thought he would make sure that Jesus was killed. But evil men cannot stop the purposes of God.

Jesus wasn't even in Bethlehem because God had warned Joseph to take Jesus and Mary to Egypt. God knew Herod would try to kill Jesus. He even told the prophet Jeremiah to write about it hundreds of years before it happened![1]

God's story of the world—His plans from before time of *Creation*, *Fall*, *Redemption*, and *Return*—cannot be stopped. He will do all that He has planned. Sickness can't stop Him, tiredness can't stop Him, storms can't stop Him, disobedient prophets can't stop Him—not even powerful, evil kings can stop Him. How very foolish it is to think that anyone or anything could stop the all-powerful God of the universe! It would be like a tiny mosquito trying to stop a lion!

God's plans for you can't be stopped either. If you are His child, His plans for you are for good—and nothing in the whole world can ever change or stop His plans for you. Whatever happens to God's children has already been in the mind and heart of God since before we were born. So we don't need to worry about anything that happens to us. God is in control, and His good plans cannot be stopped.

Like Job did, can you say to God,

> I know that you can do all things,
>   and that no purpose of yours can be thwarted.[2] (Job 42:2)

---

1. Jeremiah 31:15
2. You may need to explain that "thwarted" means stopped, opposed, prevented.

LEARNING TO TRUST GOD

✢ Read the story of Jonah. Where do you see the eye of God watching and the hand of God working in this story? If God were not all-powerful, what could have stopped God's plans? What does this tell you about God?

✢ Read Isaiah 46:9–10. What does "declaring the end from the beginning" mean? What do these verses tell you about God?

✢ *Activity:* With your family, interview an older person. Ask him or her how the hand of God has been working throughout his or her life. Where do you see things that could have stopped God's plans if He were not all-powerful? Praise God who can never be stopped!

God Is Never Surprised

Have you ever shaken your birthday presents to try to figure out what is inside? Sometimes you can figure it out, but sometimes you can't. You have to wait and be surprised. But a surprise present to you isn't a surprise to the person who gave you the gift. Why not? Because that person wrapped the gift, so he or she knows what is inside.

Do you think God is ever surprised by anything? God is never surprised because He knows everything!

> For he looks to the ends of the earth
> and sees everything under the heavens. (Job 28:24)

God sees *everything*. Nothing is hidden from His sight—not even what is inside a surprise package. He knows everything that is happening in your house right now and in your friend's house and in the whole world!

We can know about things when they happen or after they happen. But God knows about things *before* they happen!

> Behold, the former things have come to pass,
> and new things I now declare;
> before they spring forth
> I tell you of them. (Isaiah 42:9)

Before things happen—"before they spring forth"—God knows about them. Can you think of any stories in the Bible that show this is true? Maybe you are thinking about some of the following examples:[1]

1. Genesis 6:13–17; 41:25–27; Exodus 3:19; Luke 1:13; John 13:21–26; Matthew 26:34

- God told Noah to build an ark because a flood was coming.
- God gave Pharaoh a dream of skinny cows to tell him a time of bad crops was coming.
- Before Elizabeth was pregnant, God sent an angel to tell Zechariah that Elizabeth would have a baby.
- Jesus knew Judas was going to betray Him and told him to do it quickly.
- Jesus knew Peter would deny Him three times before the rooster crowed that night.

So God not only sees all things; He also *fore*sees all things. That means He sees them b*efore* they happen. God knows everything that will happen for the rest of today, next week, next year, fifty years from now, and for all time.

How can God be so sure about all these things? How could He be sure that there really would be a flood after He had Noah build the ark? God knows this for the same reason your mother knows what you are having for dinner. Why can your mother say, "We are having spaghetti and salad for supper with chocolate cake for dessert"? She can say it because she is the one who plans supper. She is in charge of supper.

So God could tell Noah there would be a flood because God is the planner of all floods. He is in charge of floods—and everything that happens in the world.

And God said to Noah, "I have determined to make an end of all flesh, for the earth is filled with violence through them. Behold, I will destroy them with the earth." (Genesis 6:13)

For behold, I will bring a flood of waters upon the earth to destroy all flesh in which is the breath of life under heaven. Everything that is on the earth shall die. (Genesis 6:17)

But there is a big difference between your mother's plans and God's plans. Your mother can't be sure that her plans won't be changed . . . but God is sure about His plans. We can plan for things to happen, but we can't make sure that they happen. But whenever God plans something, He makes sure it happens.[2] **Nothing can ever stop God's plans. So there are never any surprises for God.**

Did you know that long ago, God planned for you to be born into your family? He made your mother and father meet so they could have you. He put them in just the right place at just the right time. He works before things happen to make sure they do happen. God is a planning God who knows all things, works all things, and is never surprised by anything.

Did you know that God is already working for things that will happen to you next year . . . and twenty years from now? He already has everything taken care of—all of today and all of your tomorrows. Is there anything He can't be trusted with? Can you wake up every day knowing that God already has it planned and that nothing can happen to you that will be a surprise to Him?

---

2. You may want to teach your child the word "ordain." To ordain something is to determine something will happen and make it happen; to command it to happen and bring it about.

Great is our Lord, and abundant in power;
 his understanding is beyond measure. (Psalm 147:5)

LEARNING TO TRUST GOD

✢ Read Matthew 26:1–50. How many things can you find in these verses that Jesus knew about before they happened? What does this tell you about Jesus?

✢ Make a list of happenings in the Bible that God knew about before they happened. Then think of things in your life that God knew about before they happened. What could happen to you that would surprise God? Praise God that He knows all things, plans all things, and takes care of all things.

✢ *Activity:* Talk to your mother or father about some of the things that had to happen for you to be born. Think far back to things that had to happen in their lives and in your grandparents' lives. What does this tell you about God? With your family, write a prayer of praise to God.

God Knows What He Is Doing

Do you know that we can learn a lesson from caterpillars? They hide in cocoons for two weeks or even a few months. What is going on in that cocoon? God is at work. He is changing the caterpillar into a butterfly. Caterpillars can teach us that God is working even when we can't see what He is doing.

It is really important to remember this about caterpillars, because sometimes when we can't see what God is doing we think He isn't doing anything. Sometimes we get impatient or upset and wonder why God is not working and taking care of things. But that is wrong. God is always at work; we just might not see what He is doing.

Maybe this is the way the Hebrews felt. God had promised that He would make them a great nation . . . but they were slaves in Egypt. They were not treated well, and they had to work too hard. What about God's promise? Why wasn't He working? . . . Or was He?

Pharaoh was nervous about the many Hebrew people. He thought there were too many of them. They might try to fight his soldiers and get free. Pharaoh didn't want the Hebrew people to grow stronger. So Pharaoh ordered that whenever a Hebrew baby boy was born, the baby should be killed. Did God know about this? Would He do anything? Yes!

God was raising up a man to lead His people out of Egypt, but the Hebrews didn't know it. They didn't see what God was doing. Baby Moses—a boy—was born, but he wasn't killed. His mother hid him until he grew too big to hide. What would she do then? God was at work. He gave her the idea to make a basket for Moses and put it in the river.

Do you know what happened to Moses? The daughter of Pharaoh found Moses in the river. God made her want to keep baby Moses as her own child, making him the grandson of Pharaoh. God protected Moses from Pharaoh, who would not kill his grandson. Pharaoh's daughter even asked Moses' own mother to help take care of him.

What an amazing plan God had! Now Moses would hear about his own people. This was all part of God's good plan to free His people. All the time Moses was growing up, God was at work—even though the Hebrew people didn't know it. When Moses was a grown man, God sent him to Pharaoh to tell him God's plan to free the Hebrews.

But Pharaoh did not listen to God and did not let the Hebrew people go. Instead, he made their lives harder. He took away the straw they needed to make bricks, so that they not only had to make bricks, they had to get their own straw too.

This plan did not seem good or right. Things were worse than before. The Hebrews were angry. What was God doing? Did God make a mistake? Did He really send Moses? Would He free them? Was God really watching over the world, and was His hand at work?

God is both good and wise, so all His decisions and all His plans are right.

> For my thoughts are not your thoughts,
> neither are your ways my ways, declares the Lord.

> For as the heavens are higher than the earth,
> so are my ways higher than your ways
> and my thoughts than your thoughts. (Isaiah 55:8–9)

God was watching and working, and His plan was good and right. Even though the Hebrews did not understand what He was doing, God knew exactly what He was doing. He had a bigger and better plan than the Hebrews could imagine.

God knew that He would send all kinds of punishments on the Egyptians to show that He is a great God. When the oldest sons of all the Egyptians died, God knew that He would keep the Hebrew sons safe. The blood of a lamb on the doorframes of the houses of the Hebrew people would show that they were the people of God. Their sons would not die. The lamb's blood would keep them safe.

Yes, God would free the Hebrews and show His greatness, but even more than that He was saving them with the blood of a lamb. This helped them—and us—to understand that the blood of Jesus, the Lamb of God, saves us from our sin. God's plans were so good and so right that they were perfect. But the Hebrews didn't see all that. They only saw part of God's good plan.

We are like the Hebrews. We see only part of God's plan. It is like seeing just a few pieces of a thousand-piece puzzle. It is hard to understand what the picture will be when you only see a few pieces. So we must trust God, who sees the whole picture. He knows exactly what He is doing, and all His plans are good and right. Trust that He is watching and working perfectly . . . and remember the caterpillars.

> God thunders wondrously with his voice;
> he does great things that we cannot comprehend. (Job 37:5)

LEARNING TO TRUST GOD

✣ Read the story of the Passover in Exodus 12. How does the Passover in Egypt help us to understand about Jesus, the Lamb of God? What does this show you about the goodness of God's plan for the world?

✣ Read Isaiah 55:8–9. What does it mean that God's ways and thoughts are "higher" than ours? Can you think of a time in your life when God's way was higher than yours?

✣ *Activity:* Get a book or article about caterpillars and read about God's hidden work in cocoons. Can you see any of this from looking at the outside of the cocoon? Draw a picture of a cocoon and label it, "Sometimes God's work is hidden, but it is always good." Share with someone else what you can learn about God from caterpillars.

All for His Glory

Do you have a bike? If the chain came off your bike and someone said to you, "I'm good at fixing bikes; I can put the chain back on for you," would you think that person was showing off? No, he would be speaking the truth and being helpful. He knows that if you are going to trust him to fix your bike, you need to know that he *can* fix bikes.

God does the same thing. God does not hide His greatness and worth; He shows it off. He does not hide the truth about Himself. He shows us who He is so that we will trust Him.

> Your way, O God, is holy.
> What god is great like our God?
> You are the God who works wonders;
> you have made known your might among the peoples. (Psalm 77:13–14)

In the whole Bible we see God's mighty acts, which show us that He is great and glorious. One of God's wonders you can read about in the Bible is the amazing story of how God defeated the Midianites.

The Midianites were powerful enemies of Israel. There were so many of them and they were so strong that the Israelites actually hid from them in caves. But God told Gideon that He would give the Israelites victory over the Midianites. So the army of Israel gathered—32,000 men—to fight the Midianites. That is a big army. But the Midianite army was bigger—135,000 men! One Israelite soldier would have had to fight against 42 Midianite soldiers! Could Israel possibly defeat the Midianites?

But God loves to show His *glory*—His greatness and worth—so He told Gideon that Israel's army, not the Midianite army, was too big! He told Gideon to announce that anyone who was afraid should go home—and 22,000 men of Israel left. Now the army of Israel was only 10,000 men. Surely it would be a great victory for Israel to defeat the Midianites with only 10,000 men, and it would show that their God was great and that He was with them.

But even with an army of 10,000 men, some people might think that Israel's victory was because they were great soldiers, that they had a good battle plan, or that the Midianites were having a bad day. Then they would trust in themselves and not in the Almighty God. And God, who loves to show His glory and how great He is, wanted to make sure that everyone would know that the victory came from Him. So He told Gideon that the army had to be still smaller.

Smaller? But they were already too small to defeat such a great enemy! Yes, smaller. Do you know how small? Three hundred men. That's one Israelite soldier against 450 Midianite soldiers! Would you want to be in the army of 300? There was no way Israel could win . . . no way without God.

And just to show how great He is, God defeated the Midianites in a very strange way—with trumpets and jars! The Israelites sneaked down to the Midianite camp at night with jars over their torches and with trumpets. Gideon shouted, "For the Lord and for Gideon." The men blew their trumpets and smashed the jars, and God made the Midianites so afraid and confused that they actually fought each other! It was a great victory for the God of Israel!

Why do you think God used such a small army? So no one could think this victory came from Israel. Only God could do such a mighty wonder. If you had been there, would you cheer for the army of Israel, or for God?

> Your way, O God, is holy.
> > What god is great like our God?
> You are the God who works wonders;
> > you have made known your might among the peoples. (Psalm 77:13–14)

What god is great like our God? Why did He heal Naaman in the Jordan River? So that everyone would know *there is no God in all the earth* but the God of Israel, the one true and glorious God. Why did God use a boy to defeat a giant? To show His *glory*—His greatness and worth.

God wants us to see His greatness and worth so we will know we can trust Him—He can do anything, He is full of love and care, He knows everything, and He works for His people. His mighty acts are everywhere. Every day He causes the sun to shine, showing us that He is faithful. Every thunderstorm shows His might, and every sparrow reminds us that He cares even for little birds. If He cares for birds, He cares so much more for those who trust in Him. When we see His power in a storm, or His care—even for birds—our hearts should overflow with praise to Him. We should shout, "You are the God who works wonders! What god is great like our God?"

God wants us to see who He is. He is so wonderful, so glorious, so great, and so precious that who He is can't be hidden. A diamond sparkles because it is a diamond. When it is cut just right, the diamond can't hide the sparkle. God is like that. He is so glorious that He just "sparkles" His glory—His greatness and worth. He overflows with His glory.

All God's acts of *providence*—His providing for the world, His seeing and working in the world—show us His greatness.

> God's eye is watching and His hand is working
> to sustain and rule the world
> to work out all His plans . . .
> for His glory
> and the good of His children.

LEARNING TO TRUST GOD

✛ Read the story of the defeat of the Midianites in Judges 7. What does this story tell you about God? Is there anything in your life that is too big for God to take care of?

✛ What other wonders of God can you think of? How do they show the glory of God? Praise God for who He is.

✛ *Activity:* As a family, go to a jewelry store to look at diamonds. Ask the jeweler how diamonds are cut to show off their brilliance. God is like the best quality diamond, perfectly cut to show off the radiance and brilliance of His glory. Praise Him together as a family.

God Rules over Nature

Have you ever taken a message for someone? Maybe you answered the phone and your mother's friend asked to talk with her. If your mother wasn't home, the friend might say, "Please ask your mother to call me." When your mother gets home, you pass on the message—you tell her that her friend wants her to call. You are passing on the friend's words to your mother.

Elijah took a message too. It was a message from God to King Ahab. Ahab was a wicked king of Israel. The Bible says he was so wicked that he "did more to provoke the Lord . . . to anger than all the kings of Israel who were before him" (1 Kings 16:33). So God sent Elijah to Ahab with the message that it would not rain for years. How do you think Ahab felt about that message, and about Elijah? For sure, he was very angry. Ahab wanted to kill Elijah, but Elijah hid from him in the wilderness.

Could God keep the rain from coming for a long time? Yes, He could, and not just for a few weeks or months. God kept the rain from coming for three and a half years! By then life in Israel was very hard. The streams had dried up and the plants did not grow well, so there was very little food in Israel. God was showing His greatness. Even the rain obeys Him.

God sent Elijah to Ahab again. This time, Elijah would show Ahab and the people of Israel that God is the one true God who rules the whole world. God, who made the rain stop, would make it rain again. God is greater than all false gods. He controls all things—even rain.[1]

> He loads the thick cloud with moisture;
>   the clouds scatter his lightning.

1. 1 Kings 17–18

They turn around and around by his guidance,
    to accomplish all that he commands them
    on the face of the habitable world. (Job 37:11–12)

God rules everything in nature. Can you think of a time God showed His rule over the earth, telling it to shake? Maybe you thought of the earthquake that swallowed up Korah and others who rebelled against God, or the earthquake that shook open the prison doors for Paul and Silas.[2]

Does God rule the wind? Yes. He sent a great wind to push apart the waters of the Red Sea so Israel could walk on dry land, and He sent a wind from the sea to blow quail into the wilderness to feed the Israelites.[3] When God says, "Wind! Blow!", it blows. And when He tells it to stop, it stops.

When Jesus and the disciples were in the boat on the sea, God sent a great storm. But Jesus was asleep in the back of the boat. The disciples were scared—really scared. Some of them were fishermen who were used to storms at sea, but this was a fierce storm. The wind was blowing furiously. The waves were crashing into the boat,

2. Numbers 16:31–33; Acts 16:25–26
3. Exodus 14; Numbers 11

and the boat was starting to fill with water. What could the disciples do? They could not make the wind stop or calm the storm.

The disciples called out to Jesus, waking Him up. What did Jesus do? He looked right at that wind and said to the sea, "'Peace! Be Still!' And the wind ceased, and there was a great calm" (Mark 4:39). How did the disciples feel then? Was their fear gone? The storm was over, the waves were calm . . . but the disciples weren't calm. "They were filled with great fear and said to one another, 'Who then is this, that even the wind and the sea obey him?'" (Mark 4:41).

Who is this that even the wind and the sea obey him? He is God Almighty, the Creator and Owner of the whole world. Everything must obey His command—the wind, waves, sun, moon, stars. There is no one like Him. There is no other god besides Him. He alone rules the world. He alone is full of glory. He alone is the Most High. He alone knows the name of every star in the sky and holds the whole universe together.

> To whom then will you compare me,
>   that I should be like him? says the Holy One.
> Lift up your eyes on high and see:
>   who created these?
> He who brings out their host by number,
>   calling them all by name,
> by the greatness of his might,
>   and because he is strong in power
>   not one is missing. (Isaiah 40:25–26)

Yes, God rules everything in nature—the big things like the earth and its shaking, and the little things like birds. When Elijah was hiding in the wilderness, how did he get food? If you know the story, you know that God commanded the birds to bring him food.[4] They didn't argue or have a tantrum. Even birds must obey God's command.

---

4. 1 Kings 17:1–7

Can you believe that even tiny gnats—little tiny insects that you can hardly see—hear and obey the voice of God? He commands frogs and gnats, and even flies and locusts, too. Do you remember a story when God commanded these little creatures? He sent them to Egypt when Pharaoh would not let God's people go.[5] Surely God is great, ruling everything in His world! It all must obey Him.

What about you? Do you obey His command? We are different from the wind and the seas, the birds and the frogs. God has given us a will. Will you be like the earth and the heavens, quickly obeying His call?

> My hand laid the foundation of the earth,
>   and my right hand spread out the heavens;
> when I call to them,
>   they stand forth together. (Isaiah 48:13)

LEARNING TO TRUST GOD

- Read about God's providence over nature in one of the stories mentioned above.[6] How does this story show you God's providence over nature? What does this tell you about who God is?

- Make a list of the things in nature that the Bible shows us obey God's command. Why do you think God gave man a choice? What does that tell you about man? Pray for an obedient heart that worships God as the Ruler of all things.

- *Activity:* With your family, carefully observe something in nature. Write about your observations. What do they tell you about God? Read Romans 1:18–23. Pray as a family that you will honor God and give thanks to Him.

---

5. Exodus 8, 10
6. See footnotes for references to stories. Other evidences of God's providence over nature: Genesis 7 (rain, animals); Joshua 10 (hail, sun); Daniel 6 (lions); Jonah (wind, fish, plant).

God Rules over Life

Do you remember what we can learn from caterpillars? They teach us that God is working even when we can't see what He is doing. God's work inside the cocoon is hidden—but He is at work making a butterfly from a caterpillar.

There is another hidden work that God is doing in something that is like a cocoon—a mother's womb, where a baby is formed. God is doing this hidden work, carefully creating each person in a wonderful way. This is what the Bible says about it:

> For you formed my inward parts;
>> you knitted me together in my mother's womb.
>
> I praise you, for I am fearfully and wonderfully made.
> Wonderful are your works;
>> my soul knows it very well.
>
> My frame was not hidden from you,
> when I was being made in secret,
>> intricately woven in the depths of the earth.
>
> Your eyes saw my unformed substance;
> in your book were written, every one of them,
>> the days that were formed for me,
>> when as yet there was none of them. (Psalm 139:13–16)

Did you know that babies don't just grow alone in their mother's womb? God is right there, forming them, making them in secret! God's eye is watching and His hand is working. And every one of His works is perfect for His purposes.

Did you know that God has made you perfect for the part you have in His story of the world? God does not make mistakes. You might want to be taller or shorter, or able to do something better, but God knew just how to make you. Every day of your life is written in His book, and you were specially made for those days.

Since God makes no mistakes, we know that a baby born blind or with a hearing problem is still a special work of God. God was not careless, or sleeping, or not paying attention when that baby was growing in the mother's womb. God made that baby just as he is and as he needs to be. That baby is not an accident, but is God's special work.

Who has made man's mouth? Who makes him mute, or deaf, or seeing, or blind? Is it not I, the Lord? (Exodus 4:11)

Jesus' disciples once saw a man who had been born blind. They wanted to know what had happened. Why was the man born blind? Did his parents sin, or did he sin? Was this a punishment from God? Do you know how Jesus answered them?

Jesus answered, "It was not that this man sinned, or his parents, but that the works of God might be displayed in him." (John 9:3)

People with a weakness or "disability" have a special part to play in God's story of the world. They can show His greatness and worth in a different way than other people can. Sometimes God heals them—and that shows God's greatness. But sometimes God gives them joy, even when some things are hard for them to do. They show that God's grace is bigger than their weakness—that He helps them when things are hard.

True joy is not in having a body that works just right, but in knowing Jesus. What is important about each person is not legs that don't work right or eyes that can't see. What is most important is whether that person knows Jesus. Does that person trust Jesus as his Savior and most special Friend?

That is what is most important about every one of us. When we love and trust Jesus, we want to show God's greatness and worth to others. We believe that God is the great Ruler of the world who does everything right. He knows just what He is doing, and all His plans work out perfectly.

But if we complain about how God made us, we are saying that He made a mistake—that He should have made us taller, with a different color of hair, or better at sports or music. When we make fun of other people, we are not remembering that they are "fearfully and wonderfully made" by God. We are thinking that we are better than they are. But the Bible reminds us,

> For who sees anything different in you? What do you have that you did not receive? If then you received it, why do you boast as if you did not receive it? (1 Corinthians 4:7)

Every good thing about us was given to us by God. Only God creates life, and He has made each one of us to love Him and show His gory—His greatness and worth. Are you living for what He made you to do? Can you wake up in the morning and say to God,

I praise you, for I am fearfully and wonderfully made.
Wonderful are your works;
    my soul knows it very well. (Psalm 139:14)

LEARNING TO TRUST GOD

✟ Read Genesis 29:31–35. What does this tell you about God's providence over life? Why does God have the right to create or not create life?

✟ Read Psalm 139:1–18. What does this tell you about God? How was He watching and working when you were growing in your mother's womb?

✟ *Activity:* With your family, look at your baby pictures. Talk about how God made you—what His good and perfect gifts to you are. Thank Him that you are fearfully and wonderfully made, and ask Him to help you to show His greatness and worth.

God Rules over Rulers and Countries

When you were little, did you ever sit on someone's lap and steer the car down the driveway? When you got out of the car, did you think, "I drove the car!"? Did you really drive the car? Who really drove the car?

In some ways, we are all like little children, thinking we are driving the car. We think we are in charge, controlling things, when really God is the driver—He is controlling all things. Powerful people especially, like kings and presidents, might think they can control things. But God is really still in charge. A king might be on the throne of his country, but God is on the throne of heaven! He is the King of Kings. "For the LORD is a great God, and a great King above all gods" (Psalm 95:3).

God is the one writing the story of the world, not kings, rulers, or presidents. Do you know who decides who will be the next president? In the end, it is not the people who vote for him, but the God who rules over all things. God, not kings and rulers, is who makes countries great or weak.

The people of Israel had a king—the very best king. God was their Ruler. But they decided they wanted a man for a king, like all the other people had. Was that a good idea—to trust a man instead the all-knowing, all-powerful, good God? Did they understand that God is the best ruler of all?

It was a bad thing that Israel really didn't want God's rule. So God gave them a man as a king to teach them a lesson. This was already part of God's plan for Israel. Even before Saul was born, God had chosen Saul as the king of Israel. So God sent the prophet Samuel to crown[1] Saul as king.

---

1. Samuel anointed Saul with oil, signifying Saul's kingship. Because anointing with oil may be an unknown concept to children, the word *crown* has been used.

But Saul wasn't king for very long before he forgot that God is the greatest Ruler and all His laws are good and right. Instead of bowing to the King of Kings and obeying God as the greatest and wisest Ruler, Saul disobeyed God and did not follow God's instructions. Saul thought he could disobey the King of Kings just because he was the king of Israel.

Is it okay for anyone to disobey God? No, not even a king has the right to disobey God. A king is not greater than God. A king cannot change God's commands. A king does not know all things. Only God has the right, power, wisdom, and goodness to rule the world well. So every king and leader needs God.

But Saul did not trust God or thank God for His help. He did not have a heart that followed God.

When Saul led the army of Israel to fight against the Amalekites and won, Saul set up a statue to show his own greatness. Saul did not proclaim the greatness and worth of God. He did not give God the glory for being strong and winning over the enemy.

In the end, because Saul did not have the heart to follow God and did not want God's rule over him, God would not let him be king any longer. God was showing Israel who really is in charge and who is the Most High.

Blessed be the name of God forever and ever,
 to whom belong wisdom and might.

> He changes times and seasons;
> > he removes kings and sets up kings;
> he gives wisdom to the wise
> > and knowledge to those who have understanding. (Daniel 2:20–21)

There was another king who did not recognize God as the King of Kings. He didn't rule over Israel like Saul; he ruled over Babylon, and his name was Nebuchadnezzar. God made Babylon a great country and helped Nebuchadnezzar to build beautiful buildings. But instead of thanking and worshiping God for being the Most High, the King of all things, this is what Nebuchadnezzar said: *"Is not this great Babylon, which I have built by my mighty power as a royal residence and for the glory of my majesty?"* (Daniel 4:30).

What was wrong in Nebuchadnezzar's heart? Why does this dishonor God? No one can take away the praise that belongs to God. God is the great King over all kings. He is the one who makes kings to be kings. He is the one who makes countries strong or weak. He is the one who gives all good things. But Nebuchadnezzar did not recognize all that God did for him. Nebuchadnezzar boasted about his own greatness instead of the greatness and worth of God.

What do you think God did about that? *"While the words were still in the king's mouth, there fell a voice from heaven, 'O King Nebuchadnezzar, to you it is spoken: The kingdom has departed from you'"* (Daniel 4:31). God took away all the power, money, and respect Nebuchadnezzar had. He was no longer a great king. Now he had nothing to be proud about. He was not in charge. Even kings are ruled by God. Kings and presidents rule for only a little while. But God rules forever.

> His dominion is an everlasting dominion,
> > and his kingdom endures from generation to generation;
> all the inhabitants of the earth are accounted as nothing,

> and he does according to his will among the host of heaven
> and among the inhabitants of the earth;
> and none can stay his hand
> or say to him, "What have you done?" (Daniel 4:34–35)

It is good for us all to remember that kings and presidents are just men who God rules over. He makes them rulers, and He takes their rule away. Rulers can do only what God lets them do. They can rule only as long as God lets them. They cannot do whatever they want—no one can do that but God. Every ruler, just like every person, needs God.

> Sing praises to God, sing praises!
> Sing praises to our King, sing praises!
> For God is the King of all the earth;
> sing praises with a psalm!
> God reigns over the nations;
> God sits on his holy throne. (Psalm 47:6–8)

LEARNING TO TRUST GOD

- Read 1 Samuel 10. Where in this story do you see God's providence over rulers? Just as God chose Saul to lead Israel, God also chooses all leaders today to carry out His plan for the world. Why should this encourage you and keep you from worry? (Bonus: Read 1 Samuel 15.)

- Read Psalm 145. What does this psalm tell you about God?

- *Activity:* With your family, make a list of three to five people who rule your city, state, or country. Find one or two verses you can pray for them. Make a prayer list with these names and verses. Pray together as a family.

God Rules over His Word

Did you ever find something interesting or valuable? What did you find?

In 1947 a shepherd boy found something important. One of his sheep wandered into a cave. So he threw a rock into the cave to scare the sheep and make it run back to him. Do you know what he heard when the rock landed? He heard something break. What broke? Would you be curious to find out?

The boy was curious too. So he went into the cave and found some very old pots—and one of them was newly broken! Do you know what was inside the pots? Not water or seeds or jewels. Something more precious than jewels was inside. The boy found some very old scrolls—rolled up sheets of leather and paper-like papyrus. There were more than nine hundred scrolls or parts of scrolls. They were precious not just because there were so many or because they were more than two thousand years old, but because they were some of the earliest copies of the precious Word of God.

God's eye was watching and His hand was working so that these precious copies of His Word would be found. God sent the boy and his sheep to just the right place. He made the sheep wander into the cave. God directed the rock right into one of the pots, and then put it in the boy's mind to find out what broke. Why would He do this?

We don't know all the reasons God did this, but we do know that these scrolls, called the Dead Sea Scrolls, help to show God's providence—His watching and working—over His Word. The Bible was written by more than 40 men, and it took many, many years—1,500 years! But all the parts of the Bible fit together as one story. That is because the Bible really has one Writer—God—and men only recorded God's words.

There weren't any copy machines or printers long ago, so every copy of the Bible was written by hand. Hundreds of pages and hundreds of copies of those pages and hundreds of copies of the copies were written out by hand over many years. Do you think it would be easy for someone to make mistakes while copying the Bible? For sure! But the Dead Sea Scrolls, which contained some of the oldest copies of Scripture, showed that very few mistake were made in copying the Bible. Isn't that amazing? God has been working to guard His Word from the beginning, to make sure we always have a Bible that is the true Word of God.

> The grass withers, the flower fades,
> but the word of our God will stand forever. (Isaiah 40:8)

God is also working to make sure His Word will be known by all people everywhere. At one time there were almost no English Bibles. A person had to learn Greek, Hebrew, or another language like Latin to read the Bible. So ordinary people like us could not read the Bible.

But God put it in the heart of William Tyndale, a pastor in England, to make a Bible in English. William Tyndale wanted everyone to be able to read the Bible. But there was a problem—a big problem. It was against the law to make an English Bible! So William Tyndale was forced to leave England and go to Germany to work on his English Bible. Then, when he finished the New Testament in 1525, people wanted to burn it!

But God was watching over His Word, and fifteen thousand copies of Tyndale's English New Testament were secretly brought into England in the next five years. Now anyone who could read English could read the New Testament—even children!

William Tyndale never finished the English Old Testament because he was arrested and sent to jail. Then he was killed for putting the Bible into English. But God was still watching over His Word—His hand of providence was working to give us a Bible we can read. God had given William Tyndale a good friend named Miles Coverdale, who finished putting the Old Testament into English. God gave these men strength and courage so that we could have His Word!

The Bible is precious—so precious that it is worth dying for. Why do you think it is so precious? The Bible is the words of God Himself, the Creator and Ruler of the whole world, the One who knows and controls all things, the One whose plans never fail and who always does what He says He will do.

> For as the rain and the snow come down from heaven
> > and do not return there but water the earth,
> making it bring forth and sprout,
> > giving seed to the sower and bread to the eater,
> so shall my word be that goes out from my mouth;
> > it shall not return to me empty,
> but it shall accomplish that which I purpose,
> > and shall succeed in the thing for which I sent it. (Isaiah 55:10–11)

Rain and snow do not fall halfway to the earth and then turn around and go back into the sky! They do what God sends them to do—to water the earth so that plants grow and we have food. God's Word is the same way—it does what God sends it to do. God's Word creates faith, shows us our sin, helps us to be strong, gives us understanding, and shows us what is right. It is powerful and always does what God plans for it to do. What a precious gift the Bible is to us!

Is the Bible precious to you? Are you thankful that God watches over His Word and worked to give you a Bible you can read? Would you be willing to die so that someone could have the Bible in his own language? Do you read your Bible every day and pray that God will speak to you in His Word?

> How sweet are your words to my taste,
>   sweeter than honey to my mouth! (Psalm 119:103)

> Open my eyes, that I may behold
>   wondrous things out of your law. (Psalm 119:18)

LEARNING TO TRUST GOD

✢ Read Psalm 19:7–11. What does this tell you about God's Word? What purposes does God have for His Word?

✢ Read 2 Samuel 12:1–13. Why did God send Nathan to David? What happened when David heard God's message from Nathan? How does this story show that God watches over His Word so that it does what He has planned for it to do?

✢ *Activity:* With your family, copy some verses from the Bible. Make a copy of the copy. Repeat this several times. Did you make any mistakes in your copying? Find out what the scribes (people who copied the Bible) did to make their copies correct. What does this show you about God's providence over His Word? Is there someone your family can give a Bible to?

God Rules over Man's Heart

What happens when you are disobedient? Do you get punished? Why does a good parent punish a child? Parents discipline their children so they will learn to turn away from what is wrong and want to do what is right.

God disciplines His children for the same reason. He wants His children to love what is right and to obey His commands. How sad it is when people break God's commands and do not love what is right. That is what happened to the people of Israel living in Judah. They did not follow God or obey Him. They worshiped other gods and turned away from the one true God.

So God sent the soldiers of Babylon to fight against Judah. The Babylonians broke down the walls of Jerusalem and destroyed the beautiful temple Solomon had built. Many of the Jews—God's people—were killed. The remaining Jews were taken to Babylon (except the poorest). They had to leave the land God had given them because they disobeyed God, just like Adam and Eve had to leave the garden. What a sad day it was when they were forced to leave their homes and go to a strange country far away.

Maybe their punishment would teach them to turn from worshiping other gods. Maybe they would learn to obey God and love Him most of all.

For seventy years the people of Judah had to live in Babylon. Then King Cyrus of Persia fought against the Babylonians and won. Now he was the new king. Would the new king let the Jews of Judah go home? He had no good reason to let them go.

But we know that God rules kings. King Cyrus was not in charge. God was in charge.

> The king's heart is a stream of water in the hand of the Lord;
>   he turns it wherever he will. (Proverbs 21:1)

God was watching over His people and working for them, and this is what happened:

> The Lord stirred up the spirit of Cyrus king of Persia, so that he made a proclamation throughout all his kingdom and also put it in writing: "Thus says Cyrus king of Persia, 'The Lord, the God of heaven, has given me all the kingdoms of the earth, and he has charged me to build him a house at Jerusalem, which is in Judah. Whoever is among you of all his people, may the Lord his God be with him. Let him go up.'" (2 Chronicles 36:22–23)

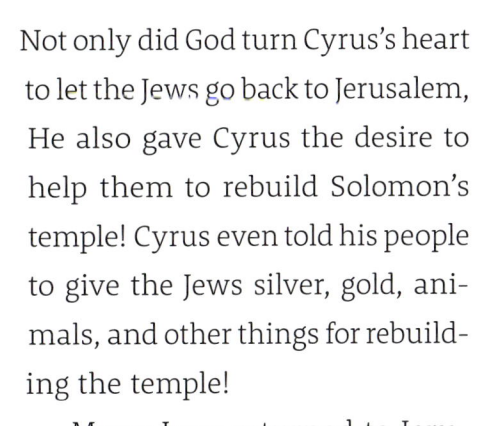

Not only did God turn Cyrus's heart to let the Jews go back to Jerusalem, He also gave Cyrus the desire to help them to rebuild Solomon's temple! Cyrus even told his people to give the Jews silver, gold, animals, and other things for rebuilding the temple!

Many Jews returned to Jerusalem and started to rebuild the temple. But then they had problems and had to stop building for 15 years. When they started building the temple again, the governor didn't know if the Jews had permission to rebuild the temple.

What could the Jews do? King Cyrus had died. Now there was a new king—King Darius. What if he wouldn't let them rebuild the temple? What if he made them leave Jerusalem again?

What could the Jews do? They could not give Darius the desire to help them. Only God could do that.

> The king's heart is a stream of water in the hand of the Lord;
>   he turns it wherever he will. (Proverbs 21:1)

Instead of getting angry or making the Jews stop building, King Darius ordered that the papers of King Cyrus should be studied. King Darius found that the Jews had been given permission to rebuild the temple. So he made a new order saying they could rebuild the temple. And he gave the Jews money and materials for rebuilding the temple too! Our God turns the hearts of men. He makes them do His will.

So the Jews kept building until the temple was finished. Then they celebrated! They were full of joy for what God had done.

> And they kept the Feast of Unleavened Bread seven days with joy, for the Lord had made them joyful and had turned the heart of the king of Assyria to them, so that he aided them in the work of the house of God, the God of Israel. (Ezra 6:22)

God does not always turn the hearts of men to do what is good. Sometimes He lets them follow what their sinful hearts want to do. Everyone is born with a sinful heart—a sinful heart that we cannot change. We cannot obey God or love what is right unless God changes our hearts. What can we do? Only God can help us.

Do you want a heart that loves God? Do you want a heart that wants to do what is right? Only God can give you that. This is what He can do:

And I will give you a new heart, and a new spirit I will put within you. And I will remove the heart of stone from your flesh and give you a heart of flesh. And I will put my Spirit within you, and cause you to walk in my statutes and be careful to obey my rules. (Ezekiel 36:26–27)

LEARNING TO TRUST GOD

✤ Read 1 Kings 12:1–24. Did God turn Rehoboam's heart to do what is good, or did God let him follow his own sinful heart? Does God have to—is He obligated to—turn man's heart away from his sin? Why not?

✤ Read Ezekiel 36:18–29. Why did God punish Israel? Why did God promise Israel a new heart?

✤ *Activity:* With your family, ask someone who you know loves God how God changed his or her heart. Where do you see God's hand of providence in this person's life?

God Rules over the Cross

If you run an errand and it takes longer than you thought it would, you might say, "I should have eaten before I left."

We say, "I should have" often. "I should have brought some money with me." "I should have packed a jacket." "I should have brought my baseball glove with me." Why do we make mistakes like this? Things happen that we don't know are going to happen. Things turn out differently from how we thought they would. There is so much we don't know.

But God never says, "I should have." God knows everything. God wrote the story of the world from beginning to end, even before the beginning. So there are no surprises to God and no mistakes in His plan. There is nothing He does not control.

However, to us it sometimes looks like there is a mistake in God's plan. That is what it looked like to the disciples when they heard Jesus talk about what would happen to Him.

> Jesus began to show his disciples that he must go to Jerusalem and suffer many things from the elders and chief priests and scribes, and be killed, and on the third day be raised. And Peter took him aside and began to rebuke him, saying, "Far be it from you, Lord! This shall never happen to you." (Matthew 16:21–22)

Peter thought this must be a mistake. Surely Jesus would not die. What about all their plans? The disciples had left everything to follow Jesus. Jesus could not die!

But Jesus knew it was not a mistake. He knew the cross was always part of God's plan. He knew that He needed to die on the cross. Jesus knew He had come to earth for this very thing—to pay for the sins of man.

When Adam and Eve disobeyed God, sin entered the world. Their sin was no surprise to God. God, who knows all things, knew they would sin. He knew that sin also brought death, hell, and separation from God—and He already had a plan to fix the sin problem.

When Adam and Eve sinned, which had already separated them from God, they tried to hide from God. But God's eye is always watching over the world, and He saw Adam and Eve trying to hide in the garden. Adam and Eve could not undo what they had done. They couldn't take care of their sin problem—only God could do that. He killed some animals, *spilling their blood*, and covered Adam and Eve with their skins. Then He promised a Savior who would defeat sin and death and end separation from God.[1]

But this was not the end of sin. Through the sin of Adam, sin spread to all men. If you plant tomatoes in your garden, then take the seeds from the tomatoes and plant them, what will you get? You won't get beans, peas, or watermelon. Tomatoes make tomato seeds that make more tomatoes. From sinful Adam came sinful men. Sinners make sinners, who make more sinners, like tomatoes make tomatoes.

God hates sin, so we cannot live forever in heaven if our sin problem is not taken care of.

Jesus knew that our sin separates us from a holy God. He also knew that God is full of love and kindness to sinners. Even though sinners deserve His

1. Genesis 3:15

punishment in hell, God made a way for sinners to be forgiven. Jesus, who never sinned, would die and *spill His blood* to cover the sin of men.

So God, who is always working in the world, planned all of history to make sure that Jesus would be born in Bethlehem; heal the blind, the lame, and the deaf; ride into Jerusalem on a donkey; be given to His enemies by a friend; and be nailed to a cross.

Even though His closest friends did not understand why Jesus had to die, Jesus knew it was God's plan from the beginning to make a way for sinners to come to God. He knew God's enemy, Satan, did not want that to happen. Even though Peter was upset and said that Jesus must not die, Jesus said to Peter:

> Get behind me, Satan! You are a hindrance to me. For you are not setting your mind on the things of God, but on the things of man. (Matthew 16:23)

He knew that the sin we all have must be paid for. He knew His blood was the payment that God had planned from the beginning of history. The cross was not a mistake; it was part of God's eternal plan—God's good plan to save sinners.

Jesus' friends—even Peter—finally understood that Jesus had to die, and that it was God's good plan from the beginning. Peter preached about this after Jesus died on the cross, rose from the dead, and went back to heaven. He said,

> Men of Israel, hear these words: Jesus of Nazareth, a man attested to you by God with mighty works and wonders and signs that God did through him in your midst, as you yourselves know—this Jesus, delivered up according to the definite plan and foreknowledge of God, you crucified and killed by the hands of lawless men. God raised him up, loosing the pangs of death, because it was not possible for him to be held by it. (Acts 2:22–24)

God's plan for the world is good and right. Sometimes, to us, it looks like there is a mistake in God's plan, but that is only because we don't understand it—like

Peter didn't understand God's plan. But God knows so much better than we do how to rule His world. When Peter preached his sermon, more than three thousand people believed in Jesus, the Savior God planned from the very beginning.

Do you trust God? Do you believe His plans are always right and that He never makes a mistake? Do you believe Jesus is the Savior who came to die for sinners?

> He himself bore our sins in his body on the tree, that we might die to sin and live to righteousness. By his wounds you have been healed. (1 Peter 2:24)

LEARNING TO TRUST GOD

- Read Romans 5:18–19. Explain these verses. Then make a chart or picture showing what these verses teach.

- Read 1 Peter 2:24 again. Explain the verse in your own words. Why was the cross a good part of God's plan? What would happen if Jesus had not died on the cross? Explain this.

- *Activity:* With your family, make a list of things that had to happen for Jesus to be the Savior. Could these things "just happen"? Where do you see God's providence—His watching and working in the world? Thank God for His good plan to send the Savior.

God Rules over Salvation

Has your family ever lost the car keys? What usually happens? Usually there is a search for the keys until they are found.

Suppose two children are asked to help to find car keys. One child is reading a book. He looks up, glances around the room, and goes back to reading his book. The other child opens drawers, takes cushions off the couch, and looks through pockets.

What is the difference in how the children are looking for the keys? One is active, taking charge, and putting a lot of energy into looking; the other is more interested in his book and isn't really looking for the keys.

God's providence over His world is more like the child who is active and taking charge. He is not just standing by, waiting for things to happen. Right now God is watching over His world and actively working in it—keeping the world going, ruling over the wind and the waves, directing animals to do His will, creating life, removing and setting up kings and presidents, and changing the hearts of men.

He is also searching—not for keys, but actively working to save people, like Zacchaeus, from their sins. Zacchaeus wanted to see Jesus, but so did many other people. That was a problem for Zacchaeus because he was short . . . and people probably did not want to help Zacchaeus to see Jesus. Do you know why?

Zacchaeus was a tax collector—he collected the money the people had to pay to the government. Many times he cheated people, making them pay too much money. So they would not visit his home or be friendly to him or let him stand in front of the crowd to see Jesus.

So Zacchaeus ran ahead and climbed a tree. Jesus could have walked by Zacchaeus and ignored him. But He didn't. He stopped and looked right at Zacchaeus. He told Zacchaeus to come down because he wanted to visit with Zacchaeus in his home. The crowd didn't like that at all! They grumbled because Jesus was going to be the "guest of . . . a sinner."

But that did not stop Jesus. He came to find sinners to save. Later that day, Jesus, who rules the hearts of men, changed the heart of Zacchaeus. Why did Jesus do this for Zacchaeus?

For the Son of Man came to seek and to save the lost. (Luke 19:10)

God is working in this world to save sinners—sinners like you, and me, and Zacchaeus . . . and another man named Saul. Saul hated Christians. He tried to find Christians and send them to jail or have them killed! But God rules over the world, seeking sinners to save, and as Saul was on his way to arrest more Christians, "suddenly a light from heaven flashed around him." And a voice spoke to him. It was the voice of God, who is actively saving lost sinners.

"Saul, Saul, why are you persecuting me?" And he said, "Who are you, Lord?" And he said, "I am Jesus, whom you are persecuting." (Acts 9:4–5)

God's eye saw Saul and His hand worked to save Saul from his sins. Saul could not turn away from the call of God. God changed his heart, and Saul put his faith in Jesus. God sent Ananias, a Christian, to help Saul and tell him what God had planned for him since before the beginning of the world.

Saul had an assignment from the rulers of the temple to arrest Christians, but God, the Greatest Ruler, had a different assignment for Saul—to seek lost sinners and preach the good news about Jesus' payment for sin on the cross. He was sent to tell them they could not work their way to heaven. Jesus had already done the work for sinners on the cross.

> But when the goodness and loving kindness of God our Savior appeared, he saved us, not because of works done by us in righteousness, but according to his own mercy. (Titus 3:4–5)

Do you think Saul had a right to be forgiven? No. No one deserves God's kindness. All of us are sinners who deserve only God's anger and punishment. But God is "rich in mercy"—He is kind to undeserving sinners like Saul and us.

Why did Jesus choose to save Zacchaeus? Why wasn't someone else in the crowd saved instead? Salvation is a gift, and God, the Giver of the gift, has the right to give His gifts to whomever He pleases.[1]

> As it is written, "Jacob I loved, but Esau I hated." What shall we say then? Is there injustice on God's part? By no means! For he says to Moses, "I will have mercy on whom I have mercy, and I will have compassion on whom I have compassion." So then it depends not on human will or exertion, but on God, who has mercy. (Romans 9:13–16)

---

1. See Matthew 22:14, John 6:44, 65; 15:16; Acts 13:48, Romans 8:29–30; 9:15–18, 21–23; Ephesians 1:3–5; 2 Thessalonians 2:13.

God has the right, power, wisdom, and goodness to rule the world well. We cannot say who should be saved. Only God has that right. Only God knows the story of the world—a story that He wrote before Creation.

Everyone is born a sinner—hating God, running away from Him, refusing to obey His commands, loving other things more than loving Him. But God, who is full of mercy, rescues some people from eternal punishment in hell. He is kind to undeserving sinners. He is still seeking and saving the lost today! God is working in His world to change hard, rebellious hearts. This is not just good news; this is the *very best* news! Do *you* think this is good news—the greatest news of all time?

> For by grace you have been saved through faith. And this is not your own doing; it is the gift of God, not a result of works, so that no one may boast. (Ephesians 2:8–9)

LEARNING TO TRUST GOD

✢ Read the story of God's work in Saul's life in Acts 9:1–19. Where do you see God's providence in this story?

✢ Read Ephesians 2:1–10. How does understanding the story of Paul's (Saul's) life help you to understand these verses? Is this your story?

✢ *Activity:* Talk with your family about how to explain Ephesians 2:1–10 to another person. Then share the good news of God's kindness to sinners with someone who is not a Christian.

God Rules over Evil

Cows give us milk. They never give us orange juice. Because cows are cows, they can give only milk. So where does chocolate milk come from? Chocolate milk comes from regular milk, made by cows, with something added to it—chocolate.

Just as only milk flows from cows, so only good flows from God because God is good.[1] Our good God made a good world—a perfect world with no sickness, sadness, suffering, or evil. But evil was added to God's good world through Satan's temptation of Adam and Eve and through their sin—just as chocolate is added to milk to make chocolate milk.[2] Now we live in a world that is not perfect. Our world is under a curse—a consequence of sin that brings sickness, suffering, death, and disasters.

But even Satan and evil are controlled by God. Nothing is outside the providence of God. Nothing is hidden from God's eye or out of the control of God's hand.

> The Lord has established his throne in the heavens,
>   and his kingdom rules over all. (Psalm 103:19)

God rules the whole world, including the evil in the world.

> Who has spoken and it came to pass,
>   unless the Lord has commanded it?
> Is it not from the mouth of the Most High
>   that good and bad come? (Lamentations 3:37–38)

---

1. Psalm 107:1
2. Note: Satan was created righteous but rebelled against God. (See Isaiah 14:12–15 and Ezekiel 28:11, 14–15—not all agree that these passages refer to Satan, but he seems at least indirectly referenced.) While God decreed the fall of Satan, He is not to be blamed for Satan's sin, for the sinner himself bears full responsibility. God has only good purposes in what he decrees and is completely good in all his ways.

> I form light and create darkness,
>   I make well-being and create calamity,
>   I am the Lord, who does all these things. (Isaiah 45:7)

God has written the history of the world, and it includes sickness, death, suffering, earthquakes, tornados, and many other evils that happen as a consequence of sin. All this has been planned and is carefully controlled by God.

How far can a dog on a leash go? Only as far as the leash reaches. Just as a dog on a leash can't go wherever it wants, so Satan can't do whatever he wants. He is stopped by God's leash. God controls Satan so Satan can do only what God allows him to do. He must have God's permission to do something.

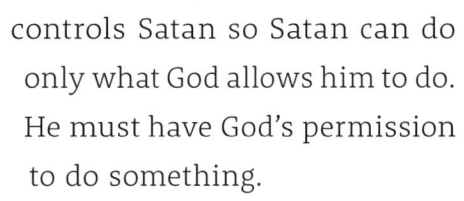

Satan thought he could prove that Job loved God only because God had been so good to Job. But Satan had to ask God if he could bring trouble to Job. God allowed Satan to bring trouble on Job, but Satan was on God's "leash."

> And the Lord said to Satan, "Behold, all that he has is in your hand. Only against him do not stretch out your hand." So Satan went out from the presence of the Lord. (Job 1:12)

Satan cannot do all the evil He wants to do, because every day God holds him back; every day God has Satan on a leash. This is God's goodness and kindness to a sinful world that deserves the horrible consequences of sin. If God allowed Satan do whatever he wanted, there would be horrible evil everywhere, all the time.

Since the fall, man was born with a sinful heart—a heart that loves evil. God, in His mercy, changes the hearts of many—like Zacchaeus and Saul—to worship Him and love what is good and right. But God's gift of salvation is not given to everyone. Not everyone loves what is good and right. If God did not have man's heart on a leash, there would be much more evil in the world. But God, in His mercy, holds back some of the evil in man's heart. God never makes anyone do bad things; sometimes He just does not stop them.[3]

God did not stop Judas from leading Jesus' enemies to Him or Pilate from giving in to the crowd who wanted to crucify Jesus. God did not stop the hands of the soldiers who nailed Jesus to the cross. He let them do what their hearts wanted to do. He opened His mighty hand that had stopped the evil in their hearts thousands of times and let them follow their stubborn, rebellious hearts. But God was still in control. He planned the cross so Jesus could save us from our sins.[4]

God is so good to stop so much of the evil that could happen in this world. And He is not bad when He does not stop it but gives us what our evil hearts want. We do not deserve His mercy. But He is so good to stop so many bad things from happening. Some people get mad at God when bad things happen. But we should thank Him every day for the bad things we deserve that *don't* happen.

God is so good to this sinful world. "All his works are right and his ways are just" (Dan. 4:37). Do you thank God for His goodness that comes to us every day?

> Oh give thanks to the Lord, for he is good,
> for his steadfast love endures forever! (Psalm 107:1)

3. Romans 1:18–25; James 1:13–14
4. Acts 2:23; 4:27

LEARNING TO TRUST GOD

✤ Read the story of God controlling Satan in Job 1:6–22. What do you know about Satan's power from this story? Explain verses 21 and 22. Why is this the right attitude toward God?

✤ Read Proverbs 16:4. Explain each phrase of the verse.[5]

✤ *Activity:* With your family, make a list of some of the bad things that could have happened this week and didn't. Did you remember to thank God for His goodness each day this week? Are you more likely to complain or to be thankful? Keep a list for a week of things you can be thankful for. Add to your list each day, and at the end of the day thank God for His goodness to you and your family.

---

5. Help your child to understand that God's creation is purposeful—that the wicked choose wickedness and that they demonstrate God's holiness when they are punished for their evil. The wicked serve God's purposes by showing His holiness and His just punishment of evil.

God Rules over Suffering

Did you get any scrapes or bruises while learning to ride a bike? You probably got a lot of them! Those scrapes and bruises hurt when you got them, but probably you hardly remember them now. You are just glad that you can ride a bike. The pain lasted only a little while, but riding a bike is something fun that you can do for years.

Joseph had pain for a while too. His 11 brothers threw him in a deep pit to die. But then they decided to sell him as a slave. He was sent far away to Egypt to work. Then his master's wife wanted him to do something wrong. When he wouldn't do it, she lied about him, and he was thrown in prison. All those things must have been very painful. You could say that Joseph got a lot of scrapes and bruises.

But God knew what He was doing. His eye was watching over Joseph and His hand was working for him. God gave Pharaoh, the king of Egypt, a dream. No one could tell him the meaning of the dream, but God showed Joseph what the dream meant.

When Pharaoh saw that God made Joseph wise, he put Joseph in charge of the whole country of Egypt. That was God's plan from the beginning. He had sent Joseph to Egypt because a time was coming when there would be little food in the place where Joseph's family lived. Since there was a lot of food in Egypt, Joseph's brothers went there to buy food. Joseph was able to help his family. He brought them all to Egypt so they would have enough to eat.

Joseph knew his brothers were wrong to sell him as a slave. But he also knew that God is in charge of all things. God rules over all things, even bad brothers. Joseph knew that God does all things right and all His plans are good. So he told his brothers,

> As for you, you meant evil against me, but God meant it for good, to bring it about that many people should be kept alive, as they are today. (Genesis 50:20)

Joseph's suffering was very hard. Being sold as a slave and going to prison is painful. But his pain was worth the good that came because of it. His family, the people of God, were kept alive. Just as scrapes and bruises seem small compared to the joy of riding a bike, Joseph's suffering—his hurts—seemed small compared to the joy of saving his family.

When you were little, the shots that the doctor gave you hurt. But they were good for you. They made you healthy. Do you think the doctor wanted to hurt you? No, but he knew you needed the medicine.

It is the same way with suffering. Suffering is always painful. But suffering brings much good. Sometimes it is hard to understand why things have to be hard, but if you are God's child, He has a good purpose in the hard things. We learn things through pain and hard times that we would not learn another way.

A woodcarver is a person who uses knives and other sharp tools to shape wood into something pretty or useful—like a wooden duck or a whistle. He cuts away the wood that is not needed. What is left is a beautiful duck or a useful whistle.

God is like a woodcarver to His people, cutting away the sins that hurt us and others. But He is creating something beautiful. He is making us to be like His Son—to be kind, trusting, patient, gentle, strong, faithful, and obedient. Sometimes the tools He uses are problems and suffering. God's carving hurts, but it is good because He is creating something beautiful in us. He is making us useful to others. The hurting is just for a while, but God's work in the lives of His people lasts forever. He is making us ready to live forever with Him in heaven.

> For this light momentary affliction is preparing for us an eternal weight of glory beyond all comparison, as we look not to the things that are seen but to the things that are unseen. For the things that are seen are transient, but the things that are unseen are eternal. (2 Corinthians 4:17–18)

We can think about the things in life that are hard—the problems and the hurts. Or we can think about the good that God does for us in the hard times. He helps us and makes us strong. He shows us that sin is ugly and heaven is beautiful. He teaches us to depend on Him and to trust Him to wipe away our tears.

No one likes pain, and suffering is hard. But we can be joyful when we remember that they make God's children trust Him more. They make us strong. Do you want to be strong? Do you want to trust God more? Don't be afraid of the scrapes and bruises in life. God, the best woodcarver, uses them to cut away the things in us that keep us from loving Him and loving others more.[1]

> Count it all joy, my brothers, when you meet trials of various kinds, for you know that the testing of your faith produces steadfastness. (James 1:2–3)

---

1. God takes no pleasure in evil. Although God ordains suffering and evil, they grieve the heart of God. (See Psalm 5:4; Lam. 3:31–33; Ezek. 18:29–32; James 1:13–15.) Moral evil does not originate in the heart of God but rather in the heart of man. Under God's sovereign decree, man follows the evil intentions of his own heart. When God ordains suffering and evil, He ordains only what is necessary and good in the big picture. A story you may want to read with your child is 2 Samuel 24:10–17. What does the punishment David chose show about the heart of God?

LEARNING TO TRUST GOD

✣ Read what Joseph told his brothers in Genesis 45:4–11. Where do you see the providence of God in these verses? What do these verses tell you about the attitude you should have toward suffering?

✣ Read Habakkuk 3:17–19. What does the Christian have that should give him joy, no matter how hard things are? Why?

✣ *Activity:* Who do you know who is suffering right now? What can your family do to encourage that person? What verses can help that person be strong? Do something practical to help that person and share your verses with him or her.

God Rules over Man's Way

Have you ever taken a hike in the woods? How do you know which way to go? Sometimes there is a path to follow, but other times there is no marked way to go. So you have to figure out the way.

There are many places where very few people live. All there is for miles around are woods, streams, and sometimes mountains. This is called the wilderness. There are no street signs in the wilderness, and it is easy to get lost. Many people hike and camp in the wilderness with the help of a guide. A guide is a person who knows the way through the wilderness and understands how to build safe fires, which plants can be eaten, and what to do in an emergency.

God is a guide too. There are many directions to go in life—some good ways and some bad. Only God knows the perfect way for us. The Bible tells us that if we trust God He will lead us in the right way.

> Trust in the Lord with all your heart,
>   and do not lean on your own understanding.
> In all your ways acknowledge him,
>   and he will make straight your paths. (Proverbs 3:5–6)

This is called "guiding providence." God's eye is watching over the way of His children and His hand is working to put them in the right way. This is what God did for Abraham's servant.

Abraham sent his servant far away to find a wife for Abraham's son, Isaac. How would the servant know who to pick? Which woman was God's choice? No human person could help the servant to make the right choice. Only God could help.

So the servant prayed and asked God to show him the right wife for Isaac. After many days of travel, Abraham's servant stopped at a well where the women would come to get water. Do you know what the servant did there? He prayed that God would point out the right wife by having the woman offer to water his camels. Only God had the wisdom to know the right wife for Isaac.

God answered the servant's prayer and caused Rebekah to get water for him and for his camels! Abraham's servant found out that Rebekah was a relative of Abraham. God had directed the servant to just the right wife for Isaac.

Do you know what the servant did then? He worshiped God.

Blessed be the LORD, the God of my master Abraham, who has not forsaken his steadfast love and his faithfulness toward my master. As for me, the LORD has led me in the way to the house of my master's kinsmen. (Genesis 24:27)

Abraham's servant could not have known that Rebekah was a relative of Abraham, or that she was the right wife for Isaac. Only God could know that. And He guided the servant to the right person.

Trust in the LORD with all your heart,
and do not lean on your own understanding.

In all your ways acknowledge him,
     and he will make straight your paths. (Proverbs 3:5–6)

God made Paul's paths straight too. Paul wanted to preach about Jesus in the region of Asia, but God had a different plan. When Paul tried to go to Asia, the Holy Spirit stopped Paul. What was God's plan? One night Paul had a vision—like a dream. In the vision a man from the country of Macedonia asked Paul to come to Macedonia to preach. Paul knew that it was God showing Him the way to go.

Even though Paul had a good plan, God had a better plan. God controls the steps of His people and directs them in the way of His story for the world.

The heart of man plans his way,
     but the Lord establishes his steps. (Proverbs 16:9)

God knew the people of Macedonia needed to hear about Jesus and His work on the cross. Paul wanted to follow God's way. So Paul changed his plans and obeyed God's plan.

Do you remember what Jonah did when God wanted him to preach in Nineveh? He went the other way. But God always finishes what He plans, and Jonah did preach in Nineveh. Jonah had to go through a storm and be in the belly of a fish before he would obey God. Isn't it better to be like Paul who wanted to obey God?

We can make our plans, but God is the one who decides which plans happen and which plans are stopped. What plans do you have for tomorrow? Are you content to change them if God stops your plans? Do you want to obey God and walk in His perfect way for you?

Come now, you who say, "Today or tomorrow we will go into such and such a town and spend a year there and trade and make a profit"—yet you do not know what tomorrow will bring. What is your life? For you are a mist that appears for a little time and then vanishes. Instead you ought to say, "If the Lord wills, we will live and do this or that." (James 4:13–15)

LEARNING TO TRUST GOD

✟ Read about God's guiding providence in Genesis 24:1–28 (or the whole chapter). Where do you see the eye and hand of God?

✟ Read James 4:13–15. Explain the verse to your parents. What heart attitude should we have toward our plans and toward God?

✟ *Activity:* Do some investigating. Find out what the Latin phrase *"deo volente"* means. How was it used? Write a letter or e-mail to someone about some plans you have. Put the initials D.V. at the end. Be ready to explain what they mean if that person should ask. Then pray that you would have a willing heart that would joyfully give up your plans for God's better plans.

God Rules over Circumstances

Suppose a father asks his son to go to the store with him. On the way to the store the father decides to drop something off at the grandparents' house. As they walk through the door, people jump out and yell, "Surprise!" The birthday party is a surprise to the son, but it isn't to the father. The father didn't "just happen" to stop at the grandparents' house. He did it on purpose.

God does things on purpose too. Things don't just happen. God makes them happen. When Jonah was thrown into the sea, the big fish didn't just happen to be at the right place at the right time. God put it there and caused it to swallow Jonah.

Pharaoh's daughter didn't just happen to be at the river at just the right time to find baby Moses. God led her there and caused her to want to take care of Moses. God works all things—all circumstances—to be part of His plan for the world. He made Pharaoh's daughter decide to go the river. He sent her to just the right spot in the river. He gave Moses' mother the idea to make a basket and put Moses in it. And He sent the basket to the same spot as Pharaoh's daughter. God plans all circumstances, every day, everywhere.

The king of Persia wanted a new queen. Of all the young women in his kingdom, who would he choose?

> Many are the plans in the mind of a man,
>   but it is the purpose of the Lord that will stand. (Proverbs 19:21)

God rules over kings and presidents. God—not the king—would choose the queen of Persia, although the king did not understand that God was in charge.

God did not choose one of the Persian women. He chose Esther, a Jew. She lived in Persia with her cousin Mordecai. When the Jews were forced to leave Jerusalem, Mordecai had been taken away to live in Persia. Because Esther's parents died, Mordecai raised her.

Of all the women in his kingdom, the king "loved Esther more" and chose her as the queen. Who made the king love Esther and choose her for his queen? Esther didn't just happen to become queen; God rules the hearts of kings and causes them to carry out His plans.[1] God had a purpose for placing Esther in the king's palace.

An evil man named Haman hated the Jews. He went to the king and asked permission to kill "a certain people" with "different laws." The people Haman wanted to kill were the "young and old, women and children . . . all Jews."

1. Proverbs 21:1

The king gave Haman permission to do whatever he wanted with these people. So Haman sent letters to every place in Persia stating that all the Jews would be killed on a certain day. Haman especially hated Mordecai and made plans to hang Mordecai.

> Many are the plans in the mind of a man,
>   but it is the purpose of the Lord that will stand. (Proverbs 19:21)

God's eye was watching over His people, and His hand was working for them. He had provided a way to save them by placing Esther in the king's palace. This is why God caused the king to choose Esther to be the queen.

Esther went to the king and asked him to spare her life and the lives of her people. When the king learned that Esther was a Jew and that Haman wanted to kill all the Jews, the king became angry. He stopped Haman's orders and even had Haman killed in the same place Haman had planned to hang Mordecai.

> Many are the plans in the mind of a man,
>   but it is the purpose of the Lord that will stand. (Proverbs 19:21)

Esther didn't just happen to be the queen. God put her there to save the Jews. Haman made his evil plans, but God had better plans. And God always does what He has planned. No one and nothing can stop God's plans.

God plans all things and controls all circumstances to make His plans happen. God has been planning all things since the beginning of the world. Nothing "just happens" in His story for the world. God is always at work in the world. His eye is watching over the world, and His hand is acting in the world every day.

God is working all the circumstances in your life too. He never makes a mistake, and there is nothing that He does not control. Nothing just happens in your life. Everything God does, He does for a good reason. What circumstances did God use to lead you to read this book right now? If He plans little things like this, do you think He also plans big and important things? His plans were made before you were born—even before the creation of the world. Our God is a great God!

> O Lord, you are my God;
> 	I will exalt you; I will praise your name,
> for you have done wonderful things,
> 	plans formed of old, faithful and sure. (Isaiah 25:1)
>
> The Lord will fulfill his purpose for me;
> 	your steadfast love, O Lord, endures forever. (Psalm 138:8)

LEARNING TO TRUST GOD

- Read Proverbs 19:21 again. Then put the verse in your own words.

- Read about the circumstances God planned so that the Ethiopian could hear the gospel in Acts 8:26–40. What circumstances were planned by God to make this happen? How was God's timing perfect?

- *Activity:* Things don't just happen. God makes them happen. With your family, plan and enjoy a special occasion—a special dinner, a surprise party, a trip to the zoo. What things can't you control? Explain why Proverbs 19:21 is true.

God's Plans Work Perfectly

What is the biggest puzzle you ever put together? Was it hard? What if you had to put together a puzzle with trillions and trillions of pieces? Could you do it?

That is what God does every day. He puts together trillions and trillions of the puzzle pieces of His providence every day! And He never makes a mistake. He never loses a piece. And all the pieces fit together perfectly.

> Great is our Lord, and abundant in power;
> his understanding is beyond measure. (Psalm 147:5)

> The counsel of the Lord stands forever,
> the plans of his heart to all generations. (Psalm 33:11)

What do you do to make it easier to put together a puzzle? Do you put all the edge pieces together first? Do you collect all the pieces of a section of the puzzle? Do you look at the picture to try to match the pieces to the right part of the puzzle?

God doesn't have to do any of those things. He doesn't need an easy way to put the pieces of the story of the world together. Sometimes He does things the hardest way—just to show His greatness and worth, to show His glory.

The prophet Micah wrote hundreds of years before the birth of Jesus that Jesus would be born in Bethlehem. To make it easy, God could have made Mary and Joseph live in Bethlehem. But He didn't. They lived in Nazareth. That seems like a piece that is out of place or doesn't fit right.

But God had all things planned perfectly.

> In those days a decree went out from Caesar Augustus that all the world should be registered. (Luke 2:1)

God, the Ruler of all things, caused Caesar Augustus to register the people—to count the people in his kingdom. Everyone had to travel to the place their family was from. This worked perfectly into God's plan to have Jesus born in Bethlehem. Mary was engaged to Joseph. Joseph was from the family of King David, who was born in Bethlehem. So Mary and Joseph had to travel to Bethlehem.

Do you know when they had to go to Bethlehem? They had to go at the time when Mary was about to give birth. God perfectly fit together Mary, Joseph, Caesar Augustus, and the king's decree so that Jesus would be born in Bethlehem—just as the prophet Micah said He would be.

What if Joseph hadn't been from the family of David? What if the timing had been wrong? What if it had been at the beginning of Mary's pregnancy instead of at the end? But there are no "what ifs" in God's providence—God's working in the world. God rules all circumstances to fit His plan. God's plans always fit together perfectly.

Wouldn't it have been easier if Mary and Joseph had lived in Bethlehem? Why did God make things work the hard way? Because the hard way shows that He is God. He is great and can do anything.

In doing things the hard way, God showed that He rules over kings and rulers; that He controls the hearts of men like Caesar Augustus; that He times things just right; that He is God and He is great.

> God's eye is watching and His hand is working
> to sustain and rule the world
> to work out all His plans . . .
> for His glory.

O Lord God, you have only begun to show your servant your greatness and your mighty hand. For what god is there in heaven or on earth who can do such works and mighty acts as yours? (Deuteronomy 3:24)

God sometimes does things the hard way so we see how great and mighty He is. Sometimes He does things in very ordinary ways so that we learn to trust Him even when it doesn't seem like He is working. But every day, in every situation, in all circumstances, God is working in the world and in your life—never making a mistake, fitting the pieces together perfectly.

Can you trust God for what is happening in your life right now? He is great and He is good. He is mighty and knows what He is doing. And He is doing it perfectly.

Trust in the Lord forever,
    for the Lord God is an everlasting rock. (Isaiah 26:4)

LEARNING TO TRUST GOD

✢ Read Joshua 10:1–14. How does this story show God's glory? Was God's timing wrong? Explain.

✢ Read Isaiah 26:4. What does it mean to trust God? With what circumstances in your life do you need to trust God?

✢ *Activity:* As a family, put together a big puzzle. Talk about the puzzle pieces of your lives while you are working on the puzzle. How do these show the goodness of God's plans?

All Things Work for Good

When all the Christmas presents are wrapped and placed under the tree, how can you tell who the presents belong to? Usually each gift has a tag with a name on it. The tag tells who the gift is for.

God's promises are like presents. They are good things given by God. One very special promise is this one:

> And we know that for those who love God all things work together for good, for those who are called according to his purpose. (Romans 8:28)

This present or promise belongs to someone. If you had to put a tag on it, whose name would you write on it? Who is this promise for? If you said, "for those who love God" or "for those who are called according to his purpose," you are right. If you are trusting in Jesus as your Savior, God promises that all things—not one or two things, but *all* things—that happen to you are for your good. This is a great present—a wonderful promise. Every single thing is for our good if we love God and Jesus is our Savior! There is *nothing* that happens to us that is not for our good.

Do you know who wrote this verse that *all things work together for good*? It was Paul. He also wrote this:

> For we do not want you to be ignorant, brothers, of the affliction we experienced in Asia. For we were so utterly burdened beyond our strength that we despaired of life itself. Indeed, we felt that we had received the sentence of death. (2 Corinthians 1:8–9)

Wait a minute! Paul suffered so much that he thought he would die? All things are supposed to be for *good!* That doesn't sound good!

It doesn't sound good . . . but it was. This is how Paul finished his writing:

> Indeed, we felt that we had received the sentence of death. But that was to make us rely not on ourselves but on God who raises the dead. (2 Corinthians 1:9)

It didn't sound good . . . but it was good. The problems Paul had in Asia taught him to depend on God. They taught him that he could trust God and that God would help him. That is a *good* thing. When we depend on ourselves, things are so much harder. But when we depend on God, we are strong because He is strong. So while it was not pleasant to suffer, it was good for Paul to learn to depend on God. The word *good* here does not mean happy and smiling all the time. *Good* doesn't mean there will be no bad news or that things won't be hard. *Good* means "good for us."

> And we know that for those who love God all things work together for good, for those who are called according to his purpose. For those whom he foreknew he also predestined to be conformed to the image of his Son. (Romans 8:28–29)

The good that God wants for us is that we would learn to be more like Jesus—that we would be more loving, patient, kind, and obedient, and we would trust God more fully. That we would depend on God and not on ourselves.

It was good that Paul learned to depend on God and get strength from him, because Paul went through many difficult things. Do you know about any of the difficulties Paul had? He was beaten many times—sometimes almost until he died. One time people threw stones at him. Three times he was in shipwrecks. He was often in danger. Many times he was hungry, thirsty, cold, and without sleep. He had many problems with the churches he was helping. He was put in prison. And one time people wanted to kill him, but his friends helped him to escape in a strange way. Do you know what they did? They let him down in a basket through a window!

Even though he had all this suffering, Paul could still say,

> And we know that for those who love God all things work together for good, for those who are called according to his purpose. (Romans 8:28)

Paul was in prison when he wrote those words. Do you know why he could say this? Because knowing Jesus was so much more precious than anything else. Being comfortable was not as good as knowing Jesus.

> Indeed, I count everything as loss because of the surpassing worth of knowing Christ Jesus my Lord. For his sake I have suffered the loss of all things and count them as rubbish, in order that I may gain Christ. (Philippians 3:8)

Paul knew that everything that happened to him was for his good. And knowing Jesus was so much better than anything else he could have—better than not being in prison, better than having good meals and good sleep, better than having people like him.

Do you believe that Jesus is precious? Do you believe that knowing and loving Him is the best treasure? If you do, then everything that happens to you is for your good. Do you want to be more like Jesus? Do you believe that God is watching over you and working for you, and that everything that happens to you is good for you to make you more like Jesus?

> God's eye is watching and His hand is working
> to sustain and rule the world
> to work out all His plans . . .
> for His glory
> and the good of His children.[1]

LEARNING TO TRUST GOD

✢ Read Romans 8:28–29 again. Explain these verses. Can you think of something that happened to you that has been for your good?

✢ Are you growing to be more like Jesus? Read Galatians 5:22–23. This is what it means to be more like Jesus. Ask God to teach you to depend on Him and be more like Jesus.

✢ *Activity:* With your family, make a booklet showing the many things that God rules. Write the providence definition from this story and the words of Romans 8:28–29 in the booklet. Then explain your booklet to someone.

---

1. This is the providence definition referred to in the Activity.

Trusting God's Heart

When you were little, did you ever spread your arms apart and say to someone, "I love you this much!"? It was your way of saying that you really loved that person.

God also has a way of saying how much He loves His children:

For as high as the heavens are above the earth,
 so great is his steadfast love toward those who fear him. (Psalm 103:11)

How far do you think the heavens are above the earth? This verse is saying that God's love for His children is really, really, really great. If you are God's child, this verse gives you the strongest reason for trusting God—He loves you! He really loves you . . . a lot. He loves you as high as the heavens are above the earth.

Sometimes we don't understand what God is doing in our lives—why something had to happen, or why He didn't make us prettier, smarter, or better at sports or music, or why things aren't different. But when we are tempted to wonder if God's ways are right, we need to remember that we can trust His *wisdom* and His *love*.

The Bible tells us about a girl who could have wondered whether God's ways are right. We don't even know her name, but we do know her story. She was a girl from Israel who was taken captive. She worked in the home of Naaman, a commander in the Syrian army. He was a very brave man, but he had a problem. He had a terrible disease called leprosy.

It was not the captive girl's choice to be a servant in Naaman's home. She could have said, "This is not fair! God made a big mistake in my life! I don't want to be here!" But God had put her there for a reason, and all His purposes are right and good. Although we do not know exactly what the young maid's attitude was, we know she had faith in God.

God was going to do a great work in Naaman's life, and He had an important part for the young girl to play in His plan. She believed God would heal Naaman. So the young girl encouraged Naaman to get help from the prophet Elisha.

Naaman did not believe in the God of Israel, but he did go to Elisha for help. Elisha told Naaman to wash in the Jordan River seven times and he would be healed. Naaman was angry at Elisha's words. He didn't want to wash in the Jordan River. But God used his servants to change his mind so that he followed Elisha's instructions.

Naaman washed in the Jordan River . . . and God healed his leprosy! Then Naaman believed that the God of Israel is the one true God. Naaman's leprosy served a good purpose—it brought him to faith in God. He saw God's greatness and worth.

But what about the young maid? God was not being unkind to her. He was working out His good purposes through her. Sometimes it is hard to understand how God is working, but we can be sure that He loves His children with an everlasting, never-ending, high-as-the-heavens love.

> For as high as the heavens are above the earth,
>> so great is his steadfast love toward those who fear him. (Psalm 103:11)

If a two-year-old found an open bottle of pills and wanted to eat them, thinking they were candy, what would a good mother do? She would take the bottle away.

Do you think the child would understand why the mother took the "candy" away? The child would not understand that the mother was acting in love. What might the child think? The child might think that the mother was mean. But the mother's heart could be trusted. She loved her child and only wanted the best for the child.

God is the very best parent of all. Even when His hand takes away something that we think is good, we can trust His heart. He always wants what is best for His children. He always acts in love toward those who have faith in Him.

> The LORD is righteous in all his ways
>> and kind in all his works. (Psalm 145:17)

God is good and wise, and He will always act in good and wise ways toward His children. The greatest good He can do for Christians is to keep them believing in and loving Him.

> I will make with them an everlasting covenant, that I will not turn away from doing good to them. And I will put the fear of me in their hearts, that they may not turn from me. (Jeremiah 32:40)

God kept this promise to the captive young maid. Even though her situation was not easy, she feared God and believed in Him. This is the greatest good—the very best thing—that God could do for her.

We can look at our situation and complain, "This is not fair! God made a big mistake in my life! I don't like this!" Or we can put our hands over our mouths, guard our hearts, and remember that God has the right, power, wisdom, and goodness to rule the world. We can trust that everything He does for His children comes from love. When you don't understand what God's hand is doing, will you trust His heart for you?

> From of old no one has heard
>   or perceived by the ear,
> no eye has seen a God besides you,
>   who acts for those who wait for him. (Isaiah 64:4)

LEARNING TO TRUST GOD

- Read Isaiah 64:4. What does this verse tell you about God's heart for His children? What does it mean to wait for God?

- Read Psalm 77:1–9. How was the psalmist feeling? Then read verses 11–15 to see how the psalmist fought to trust in God. What are some of God's faithful works he could remember?

- *Activity:* Make a list of past works of God's faithfulness to your family. Then write some verses to remind you of the goodness of God. When you have a hard time trusting God's goodness, pull out this list and read it.

Trusting God's Will

Don't be afraid. I'll catch you." Have you ever heard those words? Maybe you heard them when you were little and were afraid to go down a slide. But at the bottom of the slide stood someone you knew and loved and trusted. Hearing him or her say "I'll catch you" gave you the courage to go down the slide. You knew you could trust that person.

The same thing happened to Simon (Peter). It was morning, and Simon and some other fishermen were washing their nets. They had been fishing all night. Hour after hour they had worked their nets but caught nothing. They were tired and probably a little discouraged. It had been a tiring night with no fish to show for their hard work.

But now Jesus wanted to use Simon's boat. He asked Simon to move it out a little way from the edge of the lake. Then Jesus taught the people on the beach from the boat.

> And when he had finished speaking, he said to Simon, "Put out into the deep and let down your nets for a catch." (Luke 5:4)

How do you think Simon answered Jesus? What would you say?

Simon could have said, "Jesus, I have been a fisherman for a long time. I know a lot about fish. This is not a good time of day to catch fish." He could have said, "We're tired. We don't feel like fishing right now." Or he could have said, "We already cleaned our nets. We don't want to have to clean them again."

But Simon didn't say any of those things. Instead he said,

> Master, we toiled all night and took nothing! But at your word I will let down the nets. (Luke 5:5)

"At your word I will . . ." Simon knew that Jesus was in charge—He is the Master. Simon didn't understand Jesus' plan, but he let down the nets because Jesus told him to do so. He knew he could trust Jesus to do what was best and to know what was wise.

When Simon and the others threw their nets overboard, they caught so many fish that the nets were breaking. They filled Simon's boat with fish. But there were still more fish. So they filled the other boat with fish too.

When Simon Peter saw it, he fell down at Jesus' knees, saying, "Depart from me, for I am a sinful man, O Lord." (Luke 5:8)

When Simon saw Jesus' greatness and worth, he understood how different from Jesus he was. He was not sinless, almighty, or the ruler of all things. He couldn't command the fish or control the universe. Simon knew a lot about fishing, but Jesus knew *everything* about fishing and about everything else. Jesus is God, and Simon was only a man.

Simon and the others were ready to follow Jesus anywhere. Jesus, the very Son of God, the Ruler of the whole world, called Simon and his friends to be a different kind of fishermen. He called them to be men who would catch not fish, but the souls of men. Men who would tell others that they could trust God—that He is the Ruler of all things and is wise and good and all-powerful.

> And when they had brought their boats to land, they left everything and followed him. (Luke 5:11)

They left *everything* and followed Jesus. No excuses. No complaining. No questioning. They left *everything* and followed Jesus.

Jesus calls us to the same kind of trust in Him and obedience to Him. Instead of laying down our nets, He asks us to lay down our wills—to lay down what we want to do. He asks us to follow Him even when we don't understand what He is doing, to trust Him because He rules over everything, to believe that He is completely wise and perfect in love, and to have faith that He knows exactly what He is doing and that His ways are always right.

No excuses. No complaining. No questioning. They left *everything* and followed Jesus.

Is this the way you respond to Jesus? Do you say, "At Your word I will . . . obey my parents . . . be kind to others . . . tell the truth . . . treat others as better than myself . . . not love the world or the things of the world"? "At Your word I will . . . go where You want me to go, do what You want me to do, and be what You want me to be"? Will you say with Paul, "I will count everything as loss because of the surpassing worth of knowing Christ Jesus my Lord"[1]? Is Jesus your Master?

It is easier for us to insist on our own way, complain, or have a bad attitude. That is because we were born with sinful hearts. We cannot follow Jesus or obey His teachings without a new heart. We need the Holy Spirit to teach us to trust God and gladly bend our wills to love what He loves. We need to ask God for help.

1. Philippians 3:7–8.

Teach me to do your will,
    for you are my God!
Let your good Spirit lead me
    on level ground! (Psalm 143:10)

If you are God's child, the Holy Spirit will teach you to do God's will—first in little things, then in bigger things. Every time you obey, and every time you do things God's way, you are building a habit of following Him. Will you pray every day, "Teach me to do Your will"?

Teach me to do your will,
    for you are my God!
Let your good Spirit lead me
    on level ground! (Psalm 143:10)

LEARNING TO TRUST GOD

- Read Psalm 143:10 again. What does the verse mean by "level ground"? What commands of God are hard for you to obey? What habits of obedience and trusting in God are you forming?

- Read about Peter, the fisher of men who boldly followed Jesus, in Acts 5:17–32. What did Peter think about God's right, power, wisdom, and goodness to rule the world well?

- *Activity:* Choose one of God's commands (and ask your family to each choose one of their own) that is hard for each of you to follow. Write the command on a card. Then write Psalm 143:10 below it. Keep it where you can see it often. Each of you pray Psalm 143:10 for yourselves and each other daily. Encourage each other to trust the wisdom of God.

See God at Work

Where do spiders live? You probably didn't answer, "At the bottom of a lake," because spiders need air to breathe. But to show His greatness, God did create a spider that lives in water. It is called a water spider.[1] Do you want to know how this spider breathes in water? It is quite amazing.

The water spider catches a bubble of air with its body by doing a somersault on top of the water. It breathes this bubble of air while it spins its web under the water. When the web is finished, the water spider takes trip after trip to the top of the water to catch air bubbles to bring down to its web. He lives in this little balloon of air underwater.

> Great are the works of the LORD,
>   studied by all who delight in them. (Psalm 111:2)

God's works are great! But often we don't see His hand at work in the world; we don't see His amazing acts of providence because we are not looking for them. We don't look at the birds of the air and think about how God feeds them, or marvel at how beautifully He clothes the flowers of the fields. We don't watch thunderstorms in amazement at the power of God. It is too easy for us to rush through our days without thinking of God and His wondrous works.

But God made us to be in awe of Him. He made us to stand in amazement of who He is and what He does. He tells us to slow down, open our eyes, and see HIM.

---

1. The technical name for this spider is the *Argyroneta aquatic*, but it is commonly known as the water spider, aqua-lung spider, or diving bell spider.

I remember the days of old;
>   I meditate on all that you have done;
>   I ponder the work of your hands. (Psalm 143:5)

God is at work every day in this world. But we need to stop and see what He is doing. We need to look for His hand in all that happens and push the "off" switch on other things that grab our attention. We need to ponder, think about, and wonder about what God is doing in the world around us.

> Look at the birds of the air: they neither sow nor reap nor gather into barns, and yet your heavenly Father feeds them. (Matthew 6:26)

> Consider the lilies of the field, how they grow: they neither toil nor spin, yet I tell you, even Solomon in all his glory was not arrayed like one of these. (Matthew 6:28–29)

God is amazing! And His work is amazing! Every day, everywhere, His eye is watching over the world and His hand is working in the world.

How easy it is for us to miss the hand of God. We don't see what He is doing in His world because we are too busy looking at ourselves. We think,

How do I feel today? What do I want to do? What does this mean for me? Why me? Me, me, me.

But this is not the way we are supposed to see the world.

Looking at a flower will show us how we are to see the world. When you look at the head of a flower, what do you see?

A flower has a center with petals around it. Over and over we see this same pattern in God's universe. The solar system has a center and parts around it, just like the head of the flower. The center is the sun. The earth and all the other planets move around the sun. Even the tiny, tiny atom has the same pattern. All the parts move around the center called the nucleus.

What does this pattern point to? It points to God, the Creator and Ruler of the universe. He is the center around which everything else moves. Everything was created by God, for God, and to God—to show His greatness and worth.[2] You were created for God—to know Him, trust Him, love Him, and worship Him. You were created to see His hand at work in your life and in the world. Look for Jesus in everything in life.

Jesus is with you every single day. But sometimes we don't even notice Him. Where did you see Him today? Stop and think about your day. Did you thank Jesus for anything today? Ask for His help? Wonder at who He is? Did you see Jesus today? Behind everything in your life is Jesus.

> For from him and through him and to him are all things. To him be glory forever. Amen. (Romans 11:36)

God's eye is watching and His hand is working
to sustain and rule the world
to work out all His plans . . .
for His glory
and the good of His children.

2. See Romans 11:36.

Bless the L ORD, O my soul,
   and forget not all his benefits. (Psalm 103:2)

LEARNING TO TRUST GOD

✢ Read Psalm 103:2. Then think about the goodness of God to you today. Thank Him for His watchful eye and His working hand.

✢ Sometimes we don't understand God's work in the world because His ways are so different from ours. Read Isaiah 55:9. What does this tell you about God's ways? Can you think of an instance that shows that God's ways are higher than our ways?

✢ *Activity:* What things distract you from seeing God? What do you need to turn off or change in your life so you can meditate on Him? Go outside with your family and look at God's world. Where do you see His hand? Discover His creation together and stand in awe of the God of the universe.

God Moves in a Mysterious Way
By William Cowper

God moves in a mysterious way
His wonders to perform;
He plants His footsteps in the sea
And rides upon the storm.

Deep in unfathomable mines
Of never failing skill
He treasures up His bright designs
And works His sovereign will.

Ye fearful saints, fresh courage take;
The clouds ye so much dread
Are big with mercy and shall break
In blessings on your head.

Judge not the Lord by feeble sense,
But trust Him for His grace;
Behind a frowning providence
He hides a smiling face.

His purposes will ripen fast,
Unfolding every hour;
The bud may have a bitter taste,
But sweet will be the flower.

Blind unbelief is sure to err
And scan His work in vain;
God is His own interpreter,
And He will make it plain.

Praise for God's Providence

Sally Michael has given her life to help children and parents trust the goodness and wisdom and strength of our sovereign God. I know of no one who has more steadfastly made the majesty and mercy of God more central in ministry to children and parents. We have worked side by side in this great calling. It has been a high privilege and joy for me.

My heart soars with worship and joy and zeal as I page through Sally's new book, *God's Providence*. Here is the God I love and worship and trust. Here is absolute sovereignty and absolute goodness. Here is a foundation for life that is solid enough to sustain parents and children through the hardest times they will ever face. Here is Jesus dying and rising and reigning at the center of the greatest story in the universe. Here is a vision of God and his ways and his world that is worthy of his greatness. Here is biblical faithfulness rather than speculation. And here is practical application for children and those who love them enough to teach them.

The book could have been subtitled "Learning to Trust God." Isn't that what we want for our children—that they trust in God's sovereign love for them so deeply that they make it through fire and flood all the way to heaven, never wavering? Thank you, Sally, for pointing us so faithfully to this solid path.

—JOHN PIPER, Author; Associate Pastor for Preaching and Vision, Chancellor, Bethlehem College and Seminary

Sally Michael has written a primer on God's providence that is richly biblical and theological. This is a helpful resource for parents to introduce to their children God's constant watching and working in our world, and one that provides numerous opportunities for reflection and discussion. I heartily commend it.

—BRANDON D. CROWE, Associate Professor of New Testament, Westminster Theological Seminary

children desiring God

This storybook was adapted from *My Purpose Will Stand*, an upper-elementary Sunday school curriculum published by Children Desiring God. If you would like to further explore the providence of God or other aspects of His counsel with your student, resources are available from Children Desiring God.

Children Desiring God is a nonprofit ministry that Sally Michael and her husband David Michael helped to establish in the late 1990s. CDG publishes God-centered, Bible-saturated, Christ-exalting resources to help parents and churches spiritually train their children in the hope that the next generation will see and embrace Jesus Christ as the One who saves and satisfies the soul. Resources include nursery through youth curriculum (see sequence chart on following page), parenting booklets, and Bible memory resources. Free parenting and Christian education training audio and video lectures are also available online.

Please contact us if we can partner with you for the joy of the next generation.

childrendesiringGOD.org
cdg@desiringGOD.org

	SUNDAY SCHOOL	
Nursery	***A Sure Foundation*** A Philosophy and Curriculum for Ministry to Infants and Toddlers	
Preschool	***He Established a Testimony*** Old Testament Stories for Young Children	
Preschool	***He Has Spoken By His Son*** New Testament Stories for Young Children	

	SUNDAY SCHOOL	MIDWEEK
K	***Jesus, What a Savior!*** A Study for Children on Redemption	***He Has Been Clearly Seen*** A Study for Children on Seeing and Delighting in God's Glory
1	***The ABCs of God*** A Study for Children on the Greatness and Worth of God	***I Stand in Awe*** A Study for Children on the Bible
2	***Faithful to All His Promises*** A Study for Children on the Promises of God	(Children Desiring God will announce plans for this title in the future.)
3	***In the Beginning . . . Jesus*** A Chronological Study for Children on Redemptive History	***The Way of the Wise*** A Study for Children on Wisdom and Foolishness
4	***To Be Like Jesus*** A Study for Children on Following Jesus	***I Will Build My Church*** A Study for Children on the Church (future release)
5	***How Majestic Is Your Name*** A Study for Children on the Names and Character of God	***Pour Out Your Heart before Him*** A Study for Children on Prayer and Praise in the Psalms (future release)
6	***My Purpose Will Stand*** A Study for Children on the Providence of God	***Fight the Good Fight*** A Study for Children on Persevering in Faith
7	***Your Word Is Truth*** A Study for Youth on Seeing All of Life through the Truth of Scripture	***Abiding in Jesus*** A Study for Youth on Trusting Jesus and Encouraging Others
8	***Teach Me Your Way*** A Study for Youth on Surrender to Jesus and Submission to His Way	***Rejoicing in God's Good Design*** A Study for Youth on Biblical Manhood and Womanhood (future release)

Also by Sally Michael

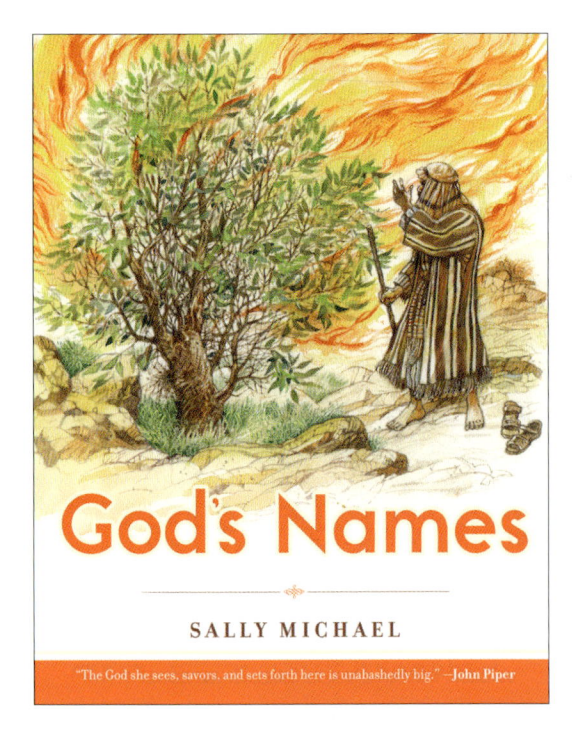

When you want to get to know someone, where do you start? How do you introduce yourself?

Usually you start with someone's name.

God knows this—and he doesn't have just one name to share with us, either! The Bible gives us many names for God and tells us what they all mean. And when we learn a new name for God, we learn something new about him, too!

This book is for you and your children to read together. Every chapter teaches something new and helps put you—and your children—on the right track in your relationship with God.

God has left his names with his people so they can know him . . . and through these pages your children can know him too.

"The God Sally sees, savors, and sets forth here is unabashedly big. Not distant and uncaring. But great enough to make his caring count."
—JOHN PIPER, Author; Pastor for Preaching and Vision, Bethlehem Baptist Church, Minneapolis, Minnesota

"Sally Michael creatively helps parents to lead their children through a fun and fascinating exploration of the various ways God's names reveal the beauty and power of his character and actions."
—JUSTIN TAYLOR, Managing Editor, *ESV Study Bible*

"Grandparents and parents and all the extended family, as well as those who make up the church of the living God, all have a divine unction to pass along God's truth to the hearts of our children! Sally Michael has given us an excellent tool in *God's Names* to do just that!"
—DOROTHY PATTERSON, General Editor, *The Woman's Study Bible*; Professor of Theology in Women's Studies, Southwestern Baptist Theological Seminary

Youth Fiction from P&R

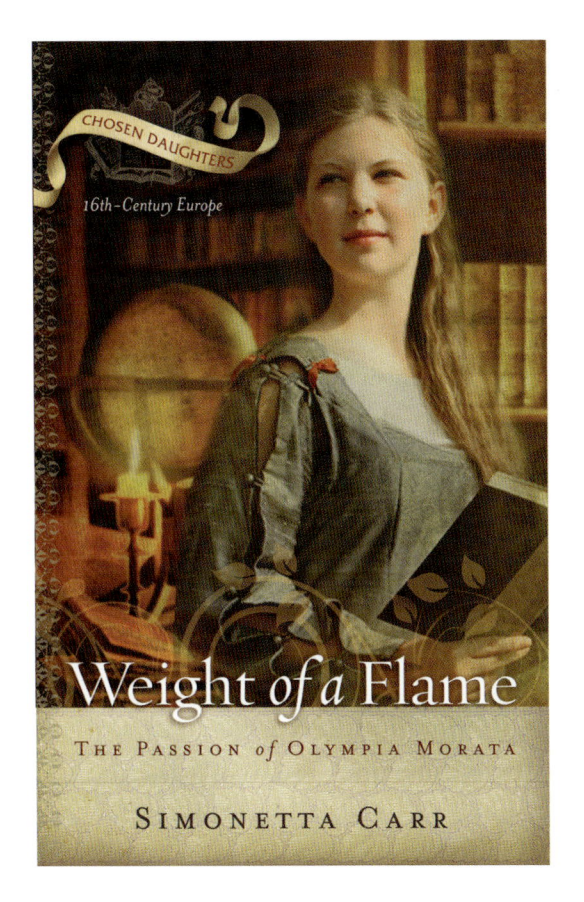

The Chosen Daughters series highlights the lives of ordinary women who by God's grace accomplish extraordinary things.

"With the precision of a scholar and the heart of a storyteller, Simonetta Carr brings to life the story of Olympia Morata, a daughter of the Italian Reformation."

—ERIC LANDRY, Executive Director of White Horse, Inc., home of *Modern Reformation* and the *White Horse Inn* radio program

Also in the Chosen Daughters series:

Against the Tide: The Valor of Margaret Wilson, by Hope Irvin Marston

A Cup of Cold Water: The Compassion of Nurse Edith Cavell, by Christine Farenhorst

Dr. Oma: The Healing Wisdom of Countess Juliana von Stolberg, by Ethel Herr

Wings like a Dove: The Courage of Queen Jeanne D'Albret, by Christine Farenhorst

Olympia Morata (1526–1555) is her father's finest student and a girl far ahead of her time. A quick tongue and a ready pen are her mind's tools to record her vivid thoughts, poetry, songs, and opinions. Appointed tutor to Duchess Renée's children, Olympia looks forward to a bright future—when suddenly, evil rumors threaten to turn her world upside down. In the midst of it all, a young doctor comes courting. Will their love survive the danger waiting on the other side of the Alps?

Youth Fiction from P&R

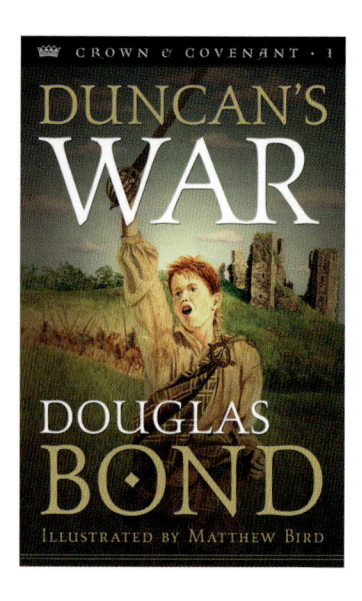

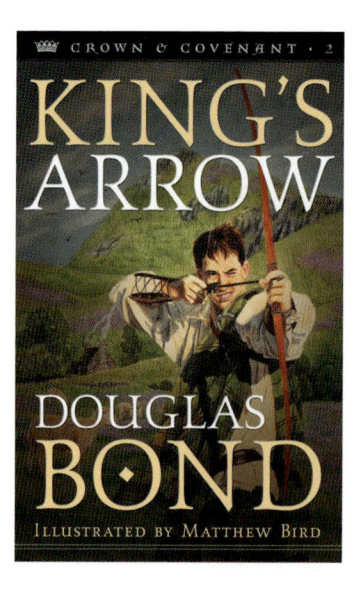

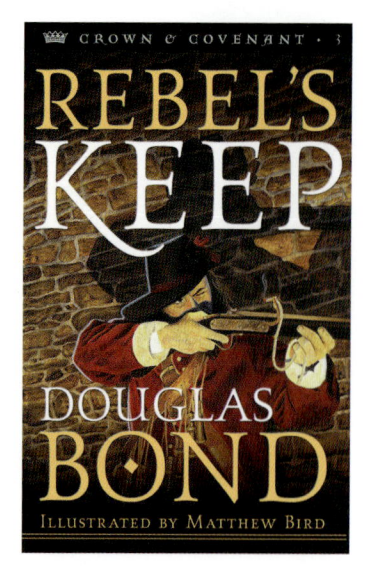

Young Duncan M'Kethe finds himself caught in the web of Sir James Turner, the former Covenanter turned military leader of the persecutors. Duncan is torn by his hatred of his enemies and his father's instructions to love them. He must be true to King Jesus while attempting to rescue his father.

The Crown & Covenant series follows the lives of the M'Kethe family as they endure persecution in 17th-century Scotland and later flee to colonial America. Douglas Bond weaves together fictional characters and historical figures from Scottish Covenanting history.

"Intrigue. Suspense. High-stakes drama. *Duncan's War* educates and inspires us to look back at heroes of the faith in awe and forward to the return of the King in joy."
—R. C. SPROUL JR., Director, Highlands Study Center

"Unleashes the reader's imagination—a rip-roaring good yarn."
—GEORGE GRANT, Director, King's Meadow Study Center

Youth Resources from P&R

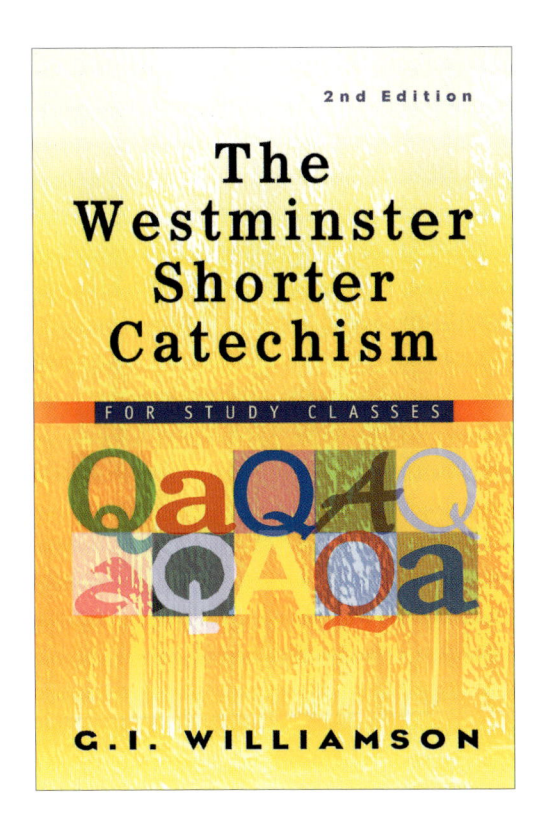

The Westminster Shorter Catechism is unrivaled as a concise and faithful summary of the central teachings of Scripture. For decades G. I. Williamson's study manuals on the Shorter Catechism have served as invaluable tools for instructing young and old in the Reformed system of doctrine.

Now newly typeset in one volume, this illustrated manual offers clear exposition of each of the 107 questions in the Shorter Catechism. Each lesson includes Scripture proofs as well as questions for review or discussion. A valuable aid for group instruction or private study, this volume has been used successfully by homeschoolers, pastors, Sunday school teachers, and parents.

Instructional Children's Fiction from P&R

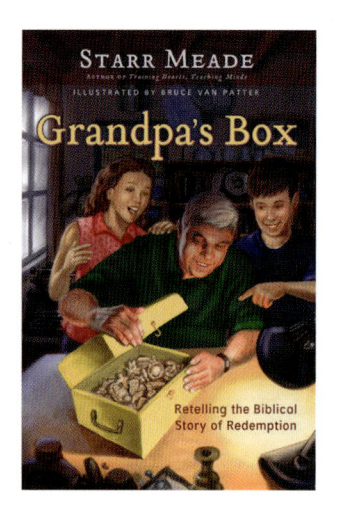

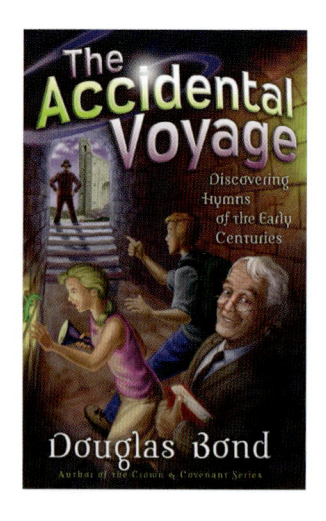

"It was a wooden box, simply made. 'I guess you could call it my war chest,' Grandpa said. As the children peered into the box, they saw many small figures—animals, people, and objects of all kinds. A number of them were carved from wood."

Learn along with Marc and Amy as Grandpa shares his stories of the great war we are all fighting. See how his special box of wooden carvings illustrates the wonderful stories of the Bible.

STARR MEADE, author of the popular *Training Hearts, Teaching Minds*, takes children to a deeper understanding of God's plan of redemption told throughout all of Scripture. Each chapter emphasizes what we learn about God, not just what we learn about individual characters in the Bible.

Follow Mr. Pipes, Annie, and Drew on another exciting adventure through mysterious lands and seas! Ride a moped with Drew through the streets of Rome, explore dark catacombs with Annie, and listen as Mr. Pipes celebrates the hymns of the early centuries. Sail with them all on a schooner bound for . . .

"Just what kind of books are the Mr. Pipes stories? Are they lessons in church history? Guides to family devotions? Unit studies on hymnody and classic ecclesiastical music? Basic theological primers? They are all these. But what is more, they are also delightful tales with memorable characters and intriguing plot twists. These are the kind of books every family is going to want to have and read—and reread."

—GEORGE GRANT, author of *Going Somewhere* and *The Christian Almanac*